The

V. S. Reid

The Young Warriors

HODDER EDUCATION

Publishing for the Caribbean
in association with
The Ministry of Education,
Jamaica

Orders: please contact Bookpoint Ltd, 130 Park Drive, Milton Park, Abingdon, Oxon OX14 4SE. Telephone: (44) 01235 827720. Fax: (44) 01235 400454. Email education@bookpoint.co.uk Lines are open from 9 a.m. to 5 p.m., Monday to Saturday, with a 24-hour message answering service. You can also order through our website: www.hoddereducation.com

© V.S Reid 1967
All rights reserved: no part of this publication may be reproduced, stored in a retrieval system, or transmitted in any form or by any means, electronic, mechanical, photocopying, recording, or otherwise, without the prior written permission of the Publishers

First published in the Blue Mountain Library Series 1967

First published in the Horizon Series 1979,
by Pearson Education Limited
Published from 2015 by Hodder Education,
An Hachette UK Company
Carmelite House
50 Victoria Embankment
London EC4Y 0DZ
www.hoddereducation.com

20 19 18 17 16 15 14 13 12 11 10 9 8
IMP 50 49 48 47 46 45

Text illustrated by Dennis Runston

Set in Baskerville

Printed and bound in Great Britain by
CPI Group UK (Ltd), Croydon, CR0 4YY

ISBN 978-0-582-76569-6

CONTENTS

Chapter One	The Questions	1
Chapter Two	The Contests	10
Chapter Three	The Hunt	23
Chapter Four	The Coney-ground	32
Chapter Five	The Redcoats	37
Chapter Six	The Mission	48
Chapter Seven	Through Enemy Lines	63
Chapter Eight	The Coming of Charlie	72
Chapter Nine	A Narrow Escape	76
Chapter Ten	Climbing the Cliff	81
Chapter Eleven	The Mocho Maroons	86
Chapter Twelve	Captured by the Redcoats	92
Chapter Thirteen	To the Rescue	96
Chapter Fourteen	Captain Dick Agrees	100
Chapter Fifteen	Outwitting the Redcoats	104
Chapter Sixteen	The Battle	113
Chapter Seventeen	Victory	118

CHAPTER ONE

THE QUESTIONS

His father's voice rolled down on him like thunder.

"Tommy! It is time to get up!"

Tommy had been dozing but now he was wide awake. He looked at the sun shining through the trees and the leaves sparkling with dew. He sprang to his feet, making sure that his knife was secure in its pouch. Tommy never slept without his knife, for he was a Maroon.

"Are you up, boy?" his father called.

"Coming, father," Tommy answered quickly.

He hurried, for that day was to be a great day in his life. That day he would begin the trials that would make him into a young warrior. It was his birthday. He was fourteen years old.

Swiftly he stooped and made his bed which was in one room of the wattle-and-daub hut his father had built. The hut had three rooms and a thatched roof.

Tommy had an unusual bed. Four logs were laid on the floor in the shape of a square. Inside the square was a layer of pimento bush, over which soft fine grass was spread. Tommy's father said this made the best bed, for it was both soft and sweet-smelling.

Tommy ran from the hut to the spring behind the great rock. He took off his clothes and dived into the pool which was at the foot of the rock. The water was so cold that it made little bumps, called goose-pimples, rise on his arms and legs. He jumped out of the pool and scrubbed himself dry and warm. Quickly he put on the pantaloons all Maroon boys wore. Then, over his chest, he slung a belt and pouch made from goatskin and fixed his knife properly in its pouch.

Although Tommy was a little ashamed to have slept so late that morning, he was proud to have finished his morning duties before his father called again. He ran from the pool into the village.

The name of the village was Mountain Top. It had two lines of huts facing each other, with a street between them. At one end of the street was the Council-house which was very large, because it was built to hold all the Maroons who lived in Mountain Top.

As he ran, Tommy looked around for his friends. Here and there he could see them running towards the centre of the village. He was glad that he was not the only one who had slept late. No doubt, on the night before, they had tossed and turned in their beds as he had done, for a long time before sleeping. No doubt, they had all been thinking about the next day when they would be made into young warriors.

At the centre of the village was the parade-ground. It was a wide place on which the Maroon warriors held their drills, their shooting-matches and their dances.

The boys ran to the parade-ground. There were four others beside Tommy and they were all about the same age as he. Older by about six months, was Charlie. Then there were David and Uriah and Tommy's best friend, Johnny. At any other time they would have been wrestling or mock-fighting, but now their faces were very serious for this was an important day.

They formed a line as they had been taught to do. Charlie stood at one end and Tommy at the other. Next to Tommy stood Johnny.

The sun was climbing above the trees. The people of the

village were now crowding about the edge of the parade-ground, leaving an open path to the closed door of the Council-house.

"Tommy," whispered Johnny, "are you afraid?"

Tommy thought for a while.

"Yes," he replied. "Are you?"

"I do not shoot well with the bow and arrow. My father will be angry," Johnny said.

"There are other things you do well," Tommy said. "You're the best runner among us all."

"But I wish I could shoot as well as you," Johnny said.

"And I wish I could run as well as you," said Tommy.

There had been a good deal of talking and laughter going on among the grown-up Maroon people, but now they had become quieter. Suddenly, the *abeng* sounded.

The abeng was the bugle of the Maroons and it was made from the horn of a cow. Its sound was low at first. Then it slowly grew louder and louder and higher. At last, it seemed as if it was racing around the treetops. The Maroons used the abeng to call up their people. It could be heard for miles around and was blown in such a way as to tell the warriors whether they were being called for a battle, or for a talk in the Council-house.

The warrior who now blew the abeng gave one last blast. They could hear the echoes going away deep into the mountains which surrounded the village. The door of the Council-house opened and the Chief of the Maroons appeared.

He was a tall, very black, handsome man. He wore a sleeveless shirt and close-fitting trousers that reached down to his ankles. His arms were muscular and around his wrist was a narrow band of gold. He carried a musket in his right hand and a powder-horn slung over his shoulder. Before stepping from the Council-house, he stood in the doorway and let his keen eyes rove over the parade-ground. Behind him came the Council consisting of the older men of the village.

The Chief and his Council walked along the open path from the meeting-house to the parade-ground where his eyes were fixed on the five boys standing in a line. Tommy was aware that Johnny was trembling beside him.

"Be brave, Johnny," he whispered, "You'll do very well." But, to tell the truth, Tommy himself felt like trembling.

Although the Chief was growing old, he still carried himself like the great warrior he had been. He had fought the English Redcoat soldiers for many, many years. The tales of his deeds were often told around the camp fires when the men went out hunting, or when the story-tellers gathered on moonlight nights in the village.

Soon the Chief reached the parade-ground. Now, no more than ten feet separated him from the boys. He halted. He looked at each in turn, beginning with Charlie. As the Chief's eyes rested upon him, Tommy felt like Brother Cockroach, in the Anancy story, when Cockroach found himself in Fowl's yard.

The Chief held up his hand and silence settled on the parade-ground. Tommy held his breath as he tried to recall everything his father had taught him. Each year, as far back as he could remember, he had seen boys made into young warriors and had dreamed of the morning when he, too, would be made into one. But he had never dreamed that he would be so afraid.

Tommy was not afraid of being hurt. What made him fearful was that he might forget the words he was supposed to say, the replies he should make to the Chief when his turn came along. But Tommy hoped he would remember. He had studied very hard.

The Chief broke the silence.

"Brothers and sisters of the Maroon people, greetings!" he said.

"Greetings, O Chief!" answered all the people.

"Today, once again, we are here to find out whether some of our boys are ready to be made into young warriors," the Chief continued. "But before we put them to the test to see how strong and active they are, we must find out how much they know of our history."

"True, true," cried the people.

Tommy could see his father in the crowd smiling at him, and suddenly he was no longer afraid. He was now sure he would remember what to say when the time came.

The Chief was facing the boys again. His face was stern.

"The first question will go to you," he said, and his finger came up fast as lightning and pointed at Uriah.

"Uriah, who are the Maroons?" he asked loudly.

"The Maroons are the brave people who hate slavery and fight for their freedom!"

The people in the crowd clapped their hands. Uriah's father was smiling. Tommy was very happy on Uriah's account. He hoped that when his time came he would answer as sharply as Uriah.

Chief Phillip looked down the line of faces again.

"Charlie," he said.

Charlie jumped when his name was called and looked wildly around. Although the morning was still cool he was sweating. Tommy knew that Charlie was afraid.

"Charlie, where do the Maroons live?"

Charlie's mouth opened but no sounds came. A groan came up from the crowd and Charlie's father looked angrily at him.

"Come on, boy," Chief Phillip said. "Speak up."

"In—in—in the mountains," Charlie stammered.

"Yes, we know. But where in the mountains?"

"In—in—Accompong."

"And where else? Speak up, boy," the Chief said.

"And—and—in Trelawny Town," Charlie replied, his eyes bulging.

"Yes. Go on, boy," Chief Phillip insisted.

"In—in—Nanny Town," said Charlie, licking his lips and trembling.

"And nowhere else?" Chief Phillip asked.

Charlie shook his head. People in the crowd began to laugh.

"And where do *you* live? Are you not a Maroon?" the Chief shouted.

Tommy felt sorry for Charlie. Although Charlie was a bully and sometimes made the smaller boys cry, Tommy thought it terrible that he was so frightened that he had forgotten where he lived.

"Yes, sir," said Charlie.

"Yes, sir, what?" asked Chief Phillip.

"I am a Maroon, sir."

"And what is the name of your village? Where do you live?"

"Mountain Top, sir."

"So, what is Mountain Top?"

Charlie was crying now. All the boys felt sorry for him. Tommy was sure that after this, Charlie would not be as rough as he used to be with the smaller boys.

Tommy suddenly realised that Chief Phillip was looking at him.

"You, Tommy," the Chief said.

"Yes, sir." Tommy spoke so loudly that the people laughed again.

Chief Phillip looked keenly at him.

"Why do the Maroons live in the mountains?" the Chief asked.

"Because, in times of war, we're like the trees of the forests," Tommy said quickly.

"What do you mean by that?"

"In times of war, our warriors clothe themselves with the branches of the trees," Tommy answered. He knew that fear had left him.

"And why do they clothe themselves in the trees of the forests?"

"So that the English Redcoat soldiers cannot see them. Our warriors become like the bush. Since we are small in numbers, we win our battles by being smart," Tommy said, holding his head high.

The people laughed and cheered and Tommy could hear his father laughing far more loudly than the others.

But now Chief Phillip held up his hand and there was silence once more. He looked at Johnny and turned his wrist, so that the gold band glittered in the sun.

"What is this on my wrist, Johnny?"

"It is a golden band that was given to our people by the King of Spain," the boy said brightly.

Tommy smiled to himself. He was happy that his best friend was not afraid.

"And why did the King of Spain give us this golden band?"

"Because we showed that we were true Jamaicans. We fought for our country."

"In what year did we begin the fighting?"

"In the year sixteen hundred and fifty-five."

"How long ago was that?" asked the Chief.

"If a warrior was born in that year, he would already have known more than eighty summers," answered Johnny.

Everybody applauded again as Chief Phillip nodded his head. The Chief turned away and looked at David.

"You, David," Chief Phillip said. "Tell us what happened in the year sixteen hundred and fifty-five."

David was a great teller of Anancy stories, but, today, he was so nervous that he found it a strain to stand still. But a Maroon boy was supposed to stand as still as a stone while he was being questioned by the Chief.

"In—in that year, the English conquered the island from the Spanish. When the Spanish fled, the English became the new rulers of Jamaica. But the Maroons were never defeated and they never left the island. So we are the true Jamaicans," David said.

"Wonderful! Wonderful!" cried the Maroons, laughing and beating the earth with their feet.

Chief Phillip held up his hand for silence and turned to Charlie once more. Somebody in the crowd tittered. Chief Phillip turned quickly. His face was stern and his fierce eyes swept over the crowd. Everybody was silent.

"Charlie," the Chief said in a soft voice, "What are the duties of a Maroon who lives in Mountain Top?"

Charlie swallowed. Clenching his hands tightly at his sides, he answered, "To—to always obey the Chief and his Council—and—and never to stray beyond our scouts."

"Why should the Chief and his Council be obeyed?"

"Because they make the law. No people or nation can become great unless they obey the law."

There was a low murmur among the Maroons. You could see them nodding their heads at the splendid way Charlie had answered the question. He was no longer a boy to be laughed at.

"And why should you never stray beyond our scouts?"

"Because although our village is in a secret place among the mountains, the Redcoats are always searching for us. And so, night and day, our scouts are always in position. They are always ready to warn us if the Redcoats should appear."

There was a burst of cheering as Charlie ended. Everybody was happy that he was no longer afraid. It was a dreadful thing for a Maroon boy to fail the questioning, for he would have to wait a whole year before he could again try to become a young warrior. Then, if he failed again, he would never become one. In times of war, he would never be trusted with important tasks.

For the first time since the questioning had begun, Chief Phillip was smiling.

"Brothers and sisters of the Maroon people, the questioning is over. And now we can all rejoice that none of the boys has failed," he cried to the Maroons. "Bring on the music while the field is being prepared for the other tests."

While their parents and the other Maroons were shouting their names and waving and laughing, the five boys remained still and solemn on the parade-ground. During their year of training, they had been warned that sharp eyes among the Council-men would be on them all through the tests. A good warrior was one who could stand unmoving for hours. In war, or in hunting, a warrior sometimes had to be as still as a tree.

A fly alighted on Tommy's nose. It sat down on the tip and rubbed its forelegs. Looking down his nose, Tommy could see it. He blinked hard, hoping it would fly away, but it only tickled him more. His nose itched. He blew a breath upward out of his mouth, but the fly seemed to like the warm air. He knew if he slapped it away with his hand, a Council-man would see him. So he stood there, while the fly jiggled and danced on his nose. Presently, it flew away but Tommy had blinked so much that tears were in his eyes. After his sight had cleared, he saw one of the Council-men grinning at him. Tommy was glad he had not moved, for he surely would have been caught.

The musicians had meanwhile entered the parade-ground. There were three drums of different sizes. The largest was taller than Tommy, and when it was struck the air trembled. There were also flutes made from bamboo. Their music was very sweet and often sad, although it could sometimes be gay. There were guitars too, and these were made from calabash gourds, neatly fixed to hardwood arms.

The band struck up a lively tune while some of the Maroons placed targets at one end of the parade-ground. The targets were four very large pieces of timber. Holes of various sizes had been made in them, the largest being wide enough for a fist to go through. The smallest hole was so narrow that only a marksman could shoot an arrow through it.

CHAPTER TWO

THE CONTESTS

CHIEF PHILLIP signalled to the band and the music ceased. One of the Council-men stepped forward. In his hand were a bow and a single sharp-pointed arrow. Everything was hushed as the Chief spoke.

"The first contest will be that of shooting," he said. "Charlie, as the oldest, you'll shoot first."

A line was marked in the dirt. Charlie stepped up to the line, with his toes just touching it. The Council-man handed him the bow and the arrow which was notched at the end where it fitted the bow-string. Charlie fixed the arrow with his right hand while his left grasped the bow and the point of the arrow together. He let his hands fall at full length as he gazed at the target. Beginning with the largest hole, he would have to shoot the arrow through all the others in turn.

Satisfied that he was ready, Charlie brought up the bow and took aim. Zing! The arrow flew straight to the target. It passed through the hole without touching. There was a shout of applause.

When the arrow was returned to him, Charlie again took aim and sent it cleanly through the second target. He shot through the third as well, and now only the smallest target was left. Not a sound was heard as he aimed for the tiny hole. Again the arrow flew through the air. But this time, as it passed through the target, the feathers at the end near the notch were torn off. Nevertheless, there were cheers for Charlie; for, in all the years, only a few young warriors had been known to send the arrow squarely through all the holes. Most had failed to do even what Charlie had done.

David and Uriah both got their arrows through the first two holes. David missed the timber altogether on the last try. Johnny did better, for he shot through the first three holes and failed only on the last. Then it was Tommy's turn.

Tommy rubbed the palms of his hands on his pantaloons before taking the bow and arrow. Then, without removing his eyes from the target, he fitted the arrow to the string. Swiftly, raising the weapon, he stretched the bow-string and relaxed his hold on the arrow. It flew straight to the target.

A second and a third time he did this. There were low voices among the Maroons; for Tommy was shooting like a marksman. They knew his father was a sharpshooter, but they did not realise that Tommy had learnt so well.

From where the shooters stood, the fourth hole was only a small black spot on the timber. It seemed impossible to send an arrow through it. But Tommy was a Maroon and he had been well trained by his father. For instance, he knew that the longer he could hold his gaze on the target, the better his aim would be. So, all during his preparations for the last and hardest shot, he never once removed his eyes from the target.

Slowly, Tommy raised the bow. His right hand drew back the arrow until his thumb touched his ear. His left hand held the bow firmly. With his left eye closed, he took aim. Then he opened the fingers of his right hand quickly and the arrow darted away.

A mighty roar went up from the Maroons, as the arrow disappeared through the hole. Not many of them had ever seen a young warrior do this before. Had it not been for the stern rules laid down by the Council, they would have rushed on to the parade-ground and lifted Tommy in the air. But on the Day of Tests, nobody was supposed to touch a Maroon boy until he had completed his tasks.

Chief Phillip held up his hands for silence. Musket, powder-horn and golden bangle glittered in the sunlight.

"Now, we will have the knife-throwing contest," the Chief said. "Prepare the targets."

There were two tests of skill in throwing the Maroon knives. In the first, the knives were thrown at a wooden target. A black dot, called a bull's eye, was painted at the centre of the target, and the people watched to see who would hit the middle of the bull's eye with the point of a knife. The five boys did well in this first test. They all hit the black dot.

But the second test was harder. In this, a naseberry was flung in the air. The boys had to throw their knives at it, so that the point stuck in the naseberry before it fell to the ground. Charlie, David and Tommy managed to cut small slices from the naseberry, and Johnny missed altogether. But Uriah sent his knife cleanly through the fruit, bearing it to the earth on its point.

"The sun was in my eye, or I would have beaten you," grumbled Charlie to Uriah, while they awaited the next contest.

"A warrior should know better than to allow the sun to shine in his eyes while he is throwing his knife," whispered Uriah.

Tommy too would have whispered a harsh word to Charlie, but Chief Phillip had turned towards them.

"Get ready for the sling-shot throwing," Chief Phillip ordered.

The boys removed their knives from the goat-skin pouches and placed them on the ground at their feet. Then they took off their belts. Each put the ends of his belt together and held them in his right hand. A Council-man came up with his hands cupped and filled with stones as large as limes. Each boy took two stones in his left hand.

Chief Phillip looked upward and chose a tall eucalyptus tree. He pointed to the top of it with his musket.

"Look at that small limb at the very top. Imagine it's a bird. Now, let me see which one of you will bring it down," he said.

Charlie, the oldest, was the first to try. Holding up the belt in his right hand, he placed the stone at the bottom of the hollow formed by the two sides. Then round and round he swung the belt, until it was singing in the wind. When it was going very fast, he let slip one end of the belt. The stone sailed upward but missed the limb by inches.

Casting with the sling-shot is not very easy even on windless days. That morning, there was a light wind blowing. It caused the tops of the trees to sway ever so slightly. One by one, the boys tried to hit the target. David came nearest to it. His stone touched the limb as it passed.

"You would have knocked out a feather, but a Maroon cannot eat feathers," said the Chief.

The Maroons laughed at the joke, but they were anxious too. Each Maroon might have had a special favourite among the five boys, but they all hoped that one of the boys would win. It would be a bad mark against the whole band of Maroons if all the boys failed.

It was time now for the last stone. The trees were still swaying in a slow dance before the wind. Charlie swung his sling, sent off the shot, and missed. So did David and Uriah. All this while, Tommy had never taken his eyes from the tree. He noticed that, after a while, he could tell when the tree had leaned out farthest.

"Why not wait until it begins to come back, before letting go the stone?" thought Tommy.

He heard the *swoosh swoosh* of Johnny's belt beside him. Johnny spun the belt and let go. He went close. But, as Chief Phillip had said, people could not eat feathers.

Tommy put the stone in the goat-skin belt. He started

swinging it slowly at first, watching the motion of the tree. He went faster as a fairly strong puff of wind came and the tree bent farther. He waited until it had bent over to the other side. Then, just before it began to straighten again, he released the stone.

Fast as a bullet it sped and hit the limb with a smack. Leaves flew all about.

"Tommy! Tommy!" yelled the Maroons.

They would have rushed on to the parade-ground had not the Council-men stopped them.

The Maroons laughed loudly. "The people of Mountain Top will never be hungry, so long as there's a hunter like Tommy!" they shouted.

"He will never be a hunter if you do not allow the contests to finish!" cried Chief Phillip. "Be silent, all of you! There is the hardest test of all to come."

At this reminder, they became quiet. For it was true that the hardest test of all was yet to come.

Chief Phillip turned to the boys. His face had lost none of its sternness, but the boys knew he was not displeased with them.

"You have all done well, indeed. But now comes the hardest test of all. Do you know what this test is?"

Tommy felt the emptiness in his stomach, but he nodded with the rest of the boys.

"What is this test? Tell us, as you have been taught," Chief Phillip said.

"It is a test of honour," all the boys said together.

"Why is it a test of honour?"

"Because we will give our word. And a Maroon warrior must never break his word."

"What is the word you will give?" asked the Chief.

The boys recited as they had been taught.

"We promise to run from here to Lookout Rock, where the stones are red as blood. We will each pick up a stone without stopping. We will run all the way back to Mountain Top."

Then they said very solemnly: "And we promise to eat nothing until we return."

"Are you hungry now?" Chief Phillip asked.

They had not eaten since they awoke. All the boys at once felt more hungry than ever.

"We are hungry now. But we shall eat nothing until we have run the five miles to Lookout Rock and returned," they replied.

"Very well," Chief Phillip said. "Be ready to go when the abeng sounds."

They turned to face the east. Far away, the sun was shining down on Lookout Rock. It was a great pink rock, the highest peak on the mountains around. The Maroons called it Lookout Rock because, in the last great Maroon War, their forefathers had spied on the English Redcoat soldiers from the top of it. The rock was beautiful in the sunlight, but Tommy and all the boys knew how hard it would be to get to Lookout Rock and return. And no matter how brave they all felt, they were very hungry.

They lined up with their faces to the east. Everything was still. They waited until the first note of the abeng was heard. Then Chief Phillip dropped his upraised hand, and off they went.

Tommy's friend, Johnny, was known as the best runner among the five. Soon after they left the village, Tommy would have raced away, following Charlie. But Johnny kept him back.

"Stay with me, Tommy," Johnny whispered. "Charlie is running too fast. He will tire soon."

So Tommy held back and ran beside Johnny. David and Uriah were running ahead of them, but had not gone as far as Charlie.

The track was level at first. The boys ran between rows

of tall cedar trees with leaves which looked like many fingers on drooping hands. Then they came to a mahogany grove where the trunks were fat and very solid. The earth, covered with fallen leaves, was as soft as a carpet under their feet.

It was chilly under the trees when they began, but the more they ran the warmer they became. After they had passed through the coffee walk that had been planted by the Maroons, they came into more open country where fruit trees grew. The track began to rise now. Tommy could smell the ripe fruit on the trees. He could smell naseberries, and custard apples, and sweetsops. They ran through a cane-field full of yellow, juicy canes. Soon, if there was no war with the Redcoats, all the Maroon people of Mountain Top would come out to reap the canes. They would boil the juice in large pots and, when it cooled, it would be turned into sugar.

But what the boys remembered most now was the taste of the ripe young canes when they chewed them in the field. Tommy felt his mouth watering as he thought of it. He glanced at Johnny and saw him licking his lips, for Johnny too, had been thinking of the taste of the canes.

"We must stop thinking about food," Johnny said.

"Yes," Tommy answered. "We must."

"Are you tired?"

"Not yet," Tommy said. "We are running very slowly."

"Oh, yes, we are. But we will pass them all on our way back," Johnny said.

"How can you be sure? They may be too far ahead of us by then," Tommy said.

"David and Uriah are doing well. But Charlie is running as if he was going ten chains, and not ten miles," said Johnny.

The boys kept their eyes and ears on the alert as they ran. There were dangers in the forest. For instance, wild boars would attack anyone who came upon them suddenly. And, like all the Maroons, the boys were always on the look-out for Redcoat soldiers.

The track had become very steep, and the earth was no longer soft. Now they were running on a rocky path, where they could be tripped by loose stones. More than one Maroon boy had in the past broken an ankle on the track.

After a while, Tommy and Johnny turned from the track and entered the bush. There were only a few large trees around, for the place was covered mostly by low shrubs. Sometimes they grew taller than the boys, but usually they were about as high as their chests. In the open places, the sun beat fiercely down on their heads. Once, Johnny grinned at Tommy, and pointed down. Tommy looked and noticed that the rocky path now had a pink colour. He knew they were nearing the foot of Lookout Rock.

Soon, the path they had taken became much steeper. They could no longer run. They were forced to scramble along. However, it levelled off again, and they picked up speed. The earth under their feet was quite pink now, but not as blood-red as it would be at the bottom of the Rock.

The boys had reached a grove of guava trees, when Johnny touched Tommy on his shoulder. They halted at once, and they stood as still as statues. This was the way of the Maroons in the bush. At the first sign of possible danger, they would become as silent as a rock.

Listening carefully, the boys heard a rustling in the bush to their right. Taking their knives from their sheaths, they dropped to their bellies on the ground. Slowly, stooping now and then to listen, they crawled towards the place from where the sounds were coming. Tommy, in the lead, soon came to a clump of mint. His keen ears told him that whatever was making the sounds would be just behind the mint-bush. Carefully, he parted the bush. And then his jaw dropped in amazement.

He turned towards Johnny, his eyes wide with surprise.

"Come and look," he whispered.

Johnny crawled quickly beside him and looked.

"It's Charlie!" he whispered. He was as surprised as Tommy.

"Sshh!" Tommy warned, his finger on his lips. "Don't say anything."

Charlie was sitting on the ground. He was eating. There was a pile of guavas beside him. David and Uriah must have taken another path and so had not seen him. Tommy and Johnny watched Charlie for a moment. Soon, he rose and began to search the ground. He picked up a stone, looked at it closely, wiped it, and then put it in his pocket. Plucking a handful of guavas from a nearby tree, Charlie left the place. But this time, he was going towards Mountain Top, instead of towards Lookout Rock.

"He broke his word!" Johnny said.

"That is not all," Tommy said slowly.

"And he turned back before he reached the Rock!"

"That's why he picked up the stone. He found a red stone which looks like the ones at Lookout Rock," Tommy said.

"What shall we do?" asked Johnny.

"I don't know," Tommy said. "I only know that we should set off again for Lookout. We are already late."

The boys began their journey again. They hadn't so much farther to go, and soon they saw the great rock quite close to them. The ground all about it was a deep red. The stones, too, were of the same colour. Without stopping, they each picked up the reddest stone they could find and turned again for Mountain Top. But, during their run back, their thoughts were all the while on Charlie. They were sad and frightened, for they had never heard of a Maroon boy breaking his word before. What were they to do?

The run was easier now since they were going downhill. Tommy saw how right Johnny had been. They were going fast but, hungry and tired though he was, Tommy knew that he could carry on at that speed straight into the village. They passed David and Uriah about a mile from the village. Tired but still cheerful, the two boys waved at Tommy and Johnny and showed them the blood-red stones.

They were almost in the village, when they heard shouting and cheering. They needed nobody to tell them the meaning of the noise. Charlie had reached the village and was being cheered as the winner of the race. When Tommy and Johnny ran in, Charlie was on the parade-ground, handing the stone to Chief Phillip. Johnny was a few yards ahead of Tommy, and David and Uriah were not far behind. The people were happy because the race had been so close. They thought that all the boys had done well.

Tommy, as he watched the Chief, felt that he looked a little too long at Charlie and at the stone Charlie had brought in. But, when the abeng sounded again, Chief Phillip raised his hand. Everybody became silent.

"The tests are over," the Chief said in a loud voice. "From this day on, until their nineteenth year, these five boys, Charlie, David, Uriah, Johnny and Tommy, are taken into the Maroon tribes as young warriors!"

A mighty roar went up from the Maroons!

The band began playing a gay Maroon dancing song. Everybody rushed forward on the parade-ground to shake the boys' hands and to say how glad they were. Each boy's father held a bow and a quiver of arrows in his hand. The quivers were made of the finest goat's skin, which was rubbed and polished until it shone.

Tommy's father kissed him on both cheeks. He handed him the beautiful new bow and arrows. Tommy drew the string and felt how smoothly the wood bent in his hand. He took out one of the arrows and held it in the air. It seemed ready to fly away out of his hand.

"Thank you, Father," Tommy said. "It is a beautiful bow. The arrows will fly straight, even if my clumsy hands do not aim them straight."

His father looked keenly at him.

"Your words tell me you are glad. But your voice is sad. Why is this, boy?"

"It is nothing, Father," Tommy replied.

"Are you sad because you did not win the race? Or the throwing of the knives?"

"I did not expect to win everything, Father, or even to win anything at all."

"Come, come, boy," his father said with a smile. "You are the best shot among the boys. Surely you expected to win the shooting?"

"I suppose so," Tommy said.

His father frowned. He thought that, for a boy who had done so well, Tommy was acting strangely.

"Well, let us go to the house. Your mother is waiting. She wants to feed you, so that you will be as fat as a pig today."

His father's words made Tommy think even harder about Charlie. He did not know what to do. He did not know whether he should tell on Charlie. After all, Charlie, by breaking his word, had shamed the whole Maroon nation. He had stopped to eat and had only pretended that he had gone to Lookout Rock. Tommy wondered whether his eyes had been playing tricks on him or whether he had really seen the Chief looking closely at the stone Charlie had given him.

Yet, if he told on Charlie, it would be very bad for the boy. They would most certainly whip him. They might even turn him out of the village. He would have to live alone in the bush.

When Tommy entered the house, his mother held him gently and kissed him. He could see tears of joy in her eyes.

"You have done well, my son. I am proud of you. One day, you'll be as great a warrior as your father."

Tommy thought that, perhaps, at this very moment, Charlie's mother was saying the same thing to her son. Telling on Charlie would hurt not only the boy but his mother and father too.

"Eat well, son," Tommy's father said. "You will be out hunting this afternoon."

It was a custom of the Maroons, that after boys had been made into young warriors, they would go on a hunt together. Of course, all Maroon boys go on hunts, but this one would be different. For the first time the boys would be out in the bush alone, without their fathers. And, what was more, they would even spend the night there.

Tommy had been given a big meal of jerked pork and roasted yams. The pork, which was the flesh of the wild boar, had been roasted over a spit, which turned slowly over a fire. It was delicious, but Tommy ate little of it. His father watched him, and said nothing.

"Rest for a while, son," his mother said when he was finished. "And you must wear this when you go out hunting later."

She gave him a sleeveless shirt. It was the same kind that was worn by the warriors. Tommy was very proud that his mother was treating him like a full warrior. But he was tired and had to rest for the big hunt. He threw himself on his bed and was soon fast asleep.

CHAPTER THREE

THE HUNT

TOMMY awoke in the afternoon. He was not used to sleeping during the day, and so, for a while, he did not know where he was. Then he remembered all the great things that had happened to him that morning. He was now a young warrior, and his mother had given him a sleeveless shirt. He was so happy that he felt like singing. He bounded out of bed, and ran outside.

The day was sunny, and drifting across the blue sky were small white clouds that looked like sheep.

"Tommy!" his mother called out to him, but he did not hear her.

She was sitting on a stool in the shade of an ackee tree, pounding cassava in a wooden mortar. When the cassava was well beaten, she would squeeze it through a coconut strainer until it was dry. Then the cassava meal would be made into bammies, which were flat, circular cakes tasting like bread.

"Tommy!" she called again.

"Yes, Mother," Tommy answered, going to her.

"Are you ready to go hunting?"

"Yes, Mother. I am going to find Johnny and the other boys."

"This is the first time you will be out hunting without your father," she said. "Will you remember all the things he has taught you?"

"I will," Tommy said.

"Very well," she said. "I have packed your knapsack. There it is, beside the door."

On the grass by the door was a fine knapsack made from the skin of a wild pig. Beside the knapsack was a water bottle, a gourd on which was carved the picture of the sun rising behind a mountain.

"Is that really for me?" he asked joyfully.

"Yes, my son," his mother said, smiling. "It's for you."

Tommy did not know what to say. For the first time he really thought about the gourd. As long as he could remember it had always hung behind the door. His father had once told him that it had belonged to his own grandfather, and had been given to Tommy's grandfather after he had been made into a young warrior.

Tommy's mother got up, walked towards him and placed her hands on his shoulder. "Look on the gourd well, my son," she said. "It existed before the first great Maroon War when your grandfather was made a young warrior. The picture of the mountain painted on it is meant to be the world, and that of the sun represented your grandfather. Now it is meant to be you, a young warrior going out into the world. You must give the world light and love, so that it will be glad of your presence. Your grandfather gave this gourd to your father when he was made a young warrior. And now your father has given it to you."

"But how can I give light to the world?" the boy asked. "The world is so big, and I am only a boy."

"Do your duty. Be kind to others. Work hard. In this way, the world will be better off because of you," his mother answered softly.

"Yes, Mother," Tommy said, trying to understand.

"Now, go. And good hunting!" his mother said.

Slowly, Tommy walked to the doorway. He took up the heavy knapsack and slung it over his left shoulder, so that it hung down his right side. He looked inside and saw that his mother had given him plenty of food. There were roasted yams and boiled sweet potatoes, still in the skin. There was a fat river mullet that had been buried in hot ashes until it was cooked. Tommy grinned and picked up the water bottle. He could look forward to a good dinner in the bush that night.

After arming himself with his knife and his bow and arrows, he said good-bye to his mother and raced away to find Johnny. Soon, all the boys were together.

The whole village had gathered to see them off. Even the band was there. And so, to the sound of music and many shouts of "Good luck! Good hunting!", the boys set off.

They entered the forest, walking one behind the other. They marched northwards, away from the village of Mountain Top. As the one who had won two of the four events in the contest, Tommy took the lead.

The Maroon village of Mountain Top was in the parish now known as St. Catherine. This was the name given to that part of the country by the English. The Maroons, of course, had their own name for the place. Tommy and his companions marched north because the English had camped to the south. The boys' plan was to follow the mountains up to Mount Diablo. The hunting was good in this part of the island.

When they were about a mile from the village, Tommy held up his hand and they all stopped. At another time, he might have given them a command to halt, but when the Maroons are hunting or at war, they scarcely speak more loudly than in a whisper. The boys sank to the ground.

The forest was very quiet and they sat in silence. They knew there were birds and little animals around them. But the "little people of the forest" were as still as they were.

Now, Tommy and his companions were only doing as their fathers had taught them. Whenever the Maroons went into the bush on a hunting trip, they always sat quietly for a while. They said that this gave the forest a chance to *know* them. If they kept as still as the trees, all the birds and little animals would come to know that they were their friends. And this would help them in their hunting.

For, you see, the Maroons knew that in hunting the coney and the wild boar, they had to move very quietly. If not, the coney and the wild boar would run away and hide. And like all the wild things in the forest, the coney and the boar would know the hunters were coming if the birds and little animals kept too quiet. So the boys sat still, and waited.

Presently, there were little noises in the bush. A tiny lizard came out from behind a rock, looked at the boys, and went back to his feeding. A mouse moved out from underneath a leaf and sat up on his hind-legs, his shiny eyes fixed on Johnny's face. Johnny winked at him. The mouse turned away and continued to eat the custard apple he had found in the grass. A canary flew out of a guava tree with a blade of grass in his mouth. Soon there were quits and humming-birds and nightingales flying about as usual. They all regarded the boys as a part of the forest. Everything was awake again.

Tommy and his companions got to their feet. They set off, walking softly, and seemed to know just how to place their feet without looking. Never once did they walk on dried leaves. They walked only where the grass was green and damp and they were careful not to make the slightest sound.

The trail they took went uphill for the most part. It would bring them to the high places where the coney lived. They would get there just at "brown-dusk", when the coneys would begin coming out to feed. The little animals would come out of their holes, slowly and softly, the tips of their noses pointing up out of their holes, as they sniffed the air. But, unless a hunter was very good with the bow, it was no use his trying to shoot them when they were so close to their hole.

It was now late in the afternoon, for the sun had sunk below the mountain. The air was becoming chilly and Tommy was glad that his mother had given him the shirt. He looked about him and was very glad that he was not alone. For, as he glanced up, he could see the tops of the great trees against the sky, and they made him feel very small. The darkness was getting closer now. Although he could not see very far in front of him, he knew that they were not lost. Soon, they would be out from among the trees and going among the rocks.

The rocks were at the top of a mountain that had been named after a great Maroon chief. He had died many, many years before Tommy was born, and was called Juan de Bolas. It was a Spanish name, pronounced Wharn de Bolas. So the mountains were called the Juan de Bolas Mountains. All the Maroons were proud of Juan de Bolas, for he had fought the English soldiers and won many battles. It was he who had been given the golden bangle which Chief Phillip now wore on his arm.

The light of day had almost gone when Tommy held up his hand. The boys halted.

"We'll rest here," Tommy said in a whisper.

"And eat, too," said David. The truth was that David was always ready to eat. He was very fat for a Maroon boy.

"True," Uriah said. "May we eat now, Chief?"

All the boys except Charlie smiled when Uriah addressed Tommy as chief. Charlie was annoyed because Tommy had been accepted as the leader of the hunt.

"He's not chief of anything," Charlie protested. "I'm older than he. I'm older than all of you."

"But he did better than all of us in the contest," David said. "That's why he has been made leader."

"I did best in the hardest test of all," said Charlie. "I won the race to Lookout Rock."

Johnny, who was sitting on the ground beside Tommy, nudged him with his elbow. But Tommy said nothing.

"All right. We won't call him Chief. We'll call him Leader," said Uriah, and added, "I'm hungry."

"Yes, Uriah. We'll eat now," Tommy said.

The boys began digging into their bags, taking out yams and potatoes, and roasted meat. As they ate, they could hear sounds of night creatures all around them. The birds had all gone to sleep, but now the crickets and the frogs were awake. The night was getting cold, for a chill wind was blowing down from the mountains. The young warriors could have lit a fire, because all Maroons carried a live coal with them whenever they went out to hunt. The coal was kept in a clay jar which was filled with sand or ashes. But they had been warned by their fathers against doing this. Nobody knew when the English Redcoat soldiers would come up into the mountains. And the boys were now far beyond the ring of Maroon scouts who guarded the village of Mountain Top.

"The moon's rising," Johnny whispered to Tommy.

Tommy looked up. The tops of the trees were beginning to look as if they had been brushed with silver. As the boys watched, the stars grew dim and the blue of the sky appeared. But it was not like the daytime blue. The sky, shining in the silver light of the moon, seemed to have been scrubbed and polished. When the light grew stronger, the sky appeared even more beautiful, and the branches of the trees became like great feathers.

Soon, the full moon rose. Tommy remembered that on that night the story-tellers would be in the village street. They would be sitting at the doorways, telling lovely old Anancy stories to the men, women and children clustered around; the old stories of smart little Brer Anancy, and the wicked Brer Tacoma, and the strong and kind Brer Bull and all the rest.

The other boys seemed to be thinking of the village too, for suddenly David spoke in a whisper:

"Once upon a time..."

David's companions drew closer to him. The moon rose higher, the wind blew softly.

"Once upon a time, Brer Anancy left his village for a far land. He walked and walked until he came to a King's house. Now Brer Anancy had walked so far, that he was very hungry and tired. So he went to the gate of the King's house and knocked on it. But nobody answered, for it was night and the guard was afraid to open the gate."

David cleared his throat, then went on:

"But Brer Anancy had the loveliest voice in the forest. And when he felt the cold wind blowing and as hungry as David (all the boys laughed softly at this) Brer Anancy began to sing.

> 'Open the gate—O
> It's never too late—O
> When to your door
> Comes the sick or the poor.'

"Now the King was a very kind man, and so, on hearing Brer Anancy's song, the gateman was afraid that the King would be angry if he heard that a poor man, or a sick man, had been turned away.

"So the guard called out to Brer Anancy: 'Which are you? The sick or the poor?'

"And Anancy answered quickly: 'I am both sick and poor.'

"So the gateman said: 'Wait, I will go and fetch the King.'"

David paused, and the other boys shuffled their feet. But they knew the good story-teller always halted in his tale for a while, so that his listeners would be anxious for him to go on.

"After some time, Brer Anancy heard the gateman returning," David went on. "The King called out, 'Who are you who comes to my palace at this late hour of night?'

"So Brer Anancy sang his little song again. The King felt very sorry for this poor, sick man with the beautiful voice and was about to order the porter to open the gate. But, just then, Brer Anancy heard a sound in the bush behind him. And, when he turned his head, there was the wicked Brer Tacoma standing in the moonlight! Brer Anancy knew that the moment the gate was opened, Brer Tacoma would rush inside the palace yard and eat the King. Now, Brer Anancy wasn't afraid of Brer Tacoma, for he knew that Brer Tacoma would not try to eat him. In the first place, Brer Anancy was too small for a real meal; and, in the second place, Brer Tacoma knew that Brer Anancy would be too smart to be eaten.

"Brer Anancy didn't know what to do. He was cold and hungry, but he knew that, as soon as the gate was opened, Tacoma would push him out of the way and pounce on the King. Brer Anancy could not bear to see the good old King killed. So, while the porter rattled the locks and chains that held the gate, Brer Anancy sang out in a loud voice:

> 'Don't open the gate!
> Or it will be too late
> If I get a push—O
> From Tacoma in the bush—O.'"

David, the story-teller, looked up at the moon. Then he

went on: "And the King understood what Anancy meant. He ordered his trumpeter to climb to the top of the wall and blow his abeng for Brer Bull. When the good and strong Brer Bull heard the abeng being blown from the palace of his friend the King, he ran out of the bush straight to the palace. And, of course, Brer Bull was too quick for Brer Tacoma. He caught Brer Tacoma before he could get away, killed him and ate him."

"And what happened to Brer Anancy?" whispered all the boys, for nice things always happened to Brer Anancy.

"Brer Anancy?" asked David. "He was taken by the King into the palace and there given all the food and rich jewels he wanted. For the King was pleased that, cold and hungry though he had been, Brer Anancy had not thought of himself first."

David ended his story and his friends chuckled with amusement.

CHAPTER FOUR

THE CONEY-GROUND

When the boys were ready to move again, they left their knapsacks where they had camped. If they had walked softly before, now they went like cats. They were now near to the coney-ground and had to watch how the wind was blowing. Only a noiseless, careful hunter could catch the coney out of its hole.

The coney uses its eyes and nose to discover its enemies. The trees stirred in the wind and, in the moonlight, cast moving shadows on the ground. The coneys' eyes were not sharp enough to notice the difference between the boys' shadows and those cast by the trees. Yet a coney's sense of smell hardly ever fails him.

Tommy and his friends knew they had to get downwind, that is, to where the wind would blow their scents away from the coney. Tommy wet his finger in his mouth, and held it up. By doing this he could feel the wind more keenly. Then he turned and led the boys to a place from which they could approach the coneys upwind.

The trees had begun to thin out, and there were now many patches of clear ground. Tommy halted. They had all been there before, hunting with their fathers. So, even at night, they knew the forest as well as we know our own town, village, or yard.

They stopped at the foot of a mahoe tree.

"We are near to the coney-ground now," Tommy said, "and had better see to our bows and knives. Let's hold a council on how we shall best catch the coneys."

"Now listen to him," Charlie jeered. "He is talking as if he's really the Chief."

"And you're talking too loud," Tommy scolded.

"Tommy is right to call a council if he wants to," Uriah said, "He's the leader."

"But there's no need for any council," Charlie protested, "We have all hunted the coney before. We all know what to do."

The boys waited to hear what Tommy would say.

"Before now, whenever we hunted in the forest, we did so with our fathers," Tommy said. "Tonight, for the first time, we are here by ourselves as young warriors. In the past, we had our fathers to think for us. Tonight, we must think for ourselves. We want to take many coneys to show the village that we are good hunters and that we are really young warriors. I say again that we should hold a council and talk about the best way to catch the coneys."

"I would like to say something," Johnny remarked. All the boys turned to him, because Johnny was not one to speak often.

"Yes, Johnny. We're listening," Tommy said.

"This morning, when we were being tested on whether we were ready to be made into young warriors, we answered questions from Chief Phillip on the history of the Maroons. We told him that, although they were small in numbers, the Maroons had won their battles because they were smart. The Maroons have always put their heads together to make plans. Tommy is smart in saying we should hold a council before the hunt."

"Oh, all right, since you all agree," Charlie said angrily.

They were all standing close together and were speaking in whispers.

"We know the way to hunt coneys," Tommy said. "We find their holes and put stones in them while the coneys are out. Then, if they become alarmed, they won't be able to find holes quickly enough. We must, therefore, remember not to try taking any coneys before stopping up the holes. We'll leave our bows and arrows and our knives, while we go into the coney-ground and find their holes."

"How will we know when we should begin to take them?" David asked.

"When I croak three times like a frog, we all return to where we left our bows," Tommy answered.

"But why should we leave our bows?" asked Charlie. "And our knives too?"

"Because we cannot crawl among the rocks with our bows in our hands. We might make a noise," Tommy said.

"But why our knives also?" Charlie asked again.

"Because I want none of us to come suddenly on a coney and try to take him before we're all ready," Tommy said. "It might scare away the others."

"Don't you trust us?" Charlie asked angrily.

Tommy remembered the race to Lookout Rock. He was tempted to say that he trusted the other young warriors but not Charlie.

"Oh, Charlie, you talk too much," Uriah said. "We know what Tommy means. Anybody coming suddenly on a coney might forget and go for him."

"Very well, Tommy," Johnny said. "You lead and tell us when to leave our bows."

Tommy went on again with the wind blowing in his face. The others followed him quietly through the clearing. Soon Tommy saw an area of stones ahead. He raised his hand and held it up for a moment. Then he brought it sharply down to his side. At once the boys began placing their bows and knives on the ground. Tommy extended both arms shoulder-high and then moved them forward until his hands met. The boys, who knew the Maroon hunting signs, went immediately on their hands and knees. When Tommy held up his clenched fist, and then opened it, they began to crawl forward.

The earth was cold and had much gravel. Tommy, at first, felt the gravel pinching into his hands and knees. But after a while he hardly noticed it. He held himself close to the ground, moving just a little at a time. His eyes searched the ground for holes, which, he knew, were usually behind the larger rocks. Whenever the rocks were in shadow, he groped with his hands. About a minute after he had begun searching, he found the first hole. He sealed it by poking a stone into it. He was now well inside the coney-ground, and the holes were increasing in number. He had just finished jamming a stone into a large hole, when he saw his first coney.

Tommy was pleased that he had been moving so softly that he could almost have reached out and touched the coney. It was very fat and may have come from the hole he had just stopped. In the moonlight its coat appeared pearl-grey in colour. It was sitting with its two little ears whisking back and forth and its nose in the air, wriggling about for a scent. Then all of a sudden it was not there. Coneys could escape very quickly, especially when there are many stones for them to hide behind.

Tommy waited a while before going on. He was amused at the speed at which the coney had moved, and wondered whether the other boys were having a similar experience.

All the boys had, like Tommy, come suddenly upon coneys. Charlie might have taken a chance at getting one of them. But it would have squeaked in alarm. Since all the holes had not yet been stopped, the other coneys would have bolted into them and the hunt would have failed.

Soon, Tommy knew they had gone right through the coney-ground, for the trees began to increase in number. Three times, he croaked like a frog and went back to where they had left the bows.

"Everybody here?" asked Tommy when they were together again. "Johnny? David? Uriah? Charlie?"

All the boys had got back.

"Well, we'll go in now. But just one thing. We don't all have to use the bow. Each will use the weapon he can handle best," Tommy said. "Uriah and Charlie, you're better at knives, so you'll use those. David, you will hunt with stones. Johnny and I will use our bows."

"And why can't I use the bow too?" Charlie grumbled.

"Because we don't want you to shoot us instead of the coney, you marksman, you," David said, mocking him.

The boys chuckled softly as they moved off. They went silently about their work, for they knew that the people at Mountain Top needed the food the coneys provided. The Maroons lived by hunting. And so, although the trip was a sort of reward to the boys for having done well at the tests, it was also a serious hunting trip to add to the food supply for the village. The only sounds that could be heard were the swish of an arrow, the whistle of a knife, or the thud of the stones thrown by David with a skill almost as great as that of his namesake in the Bible. Now and again, there was a squeak from a coney, but the boys were such good hunters that the coneys never knew they were being hunted until it was too late.

When the few that got away had vanished, Tommy gave the frog's croak again. The boys came up to him panting. It had been tough work going through the rocks.

"Let us gather up what we have now and go back to camp," Tommy said. "The moon's going down. Even if they come back tonight, we won't be able to see them."

"Yes. And we'll have to be off early in the morning," Uriah said.

The boys gathered the coneys and packed them in the bags they had brought. Then they returned where they had camped to eat, and where David had told his Anancy story. After gathering branches and scattered leaves, they made a great mound under the trees. Into this they burrowed. Soon they were as snug and warm as if they were at home in their beds. Tired as they were, they soon fell asleep.

CHAPTER FIVE

THE REDCOATS

TOMMY awoke as the first light of dawn appeared under the trees. He sat up and rubbed his eyes, the leaves falling from his chest and shoulders. Beside him, Johnny was also stirring. Then, one by one, the other young hunters awoke and sat up, shaking the leaves from their bodies like puppies after a shower. Uriah had a leaf sticking in one nostril and another in an ear. David saw them, pointed his finger at Uriah and burst out laughing. Then as they looked closely at each other and saw how the leaves and burrs had stuck all over their heads and faces, they had a good laugh together.

As they laughed, however, they were busy getting their things together. They were about to go deeper into the mountains, to the place they called Pimento Walk, to hunt birds. As soon as everybody was ready, Tommy led the way. This time, they turned east. They had left the bags of coneys under some leaves, well covered with stones.

The boys trotted most of the way. By the time the sun was peeping over the mountains of the place we now know as Sligoville, they were in Pimento Walk.

Pimento Walk was a great grove of pimento trees and was a favourite feeding ground for white-wings, baldpates and pigeons. While they were on their way, the boys had been plucking branches from the trees that they passed. They draped these all over themselves and, in a short while, they were like walking trees. Every young warrior was hidden under branches. Only their hands were left uncovered.

At a signal from Tommy, they separated, each going to the place of his own choice. In a moment all was still, and the boys waited. Then the birds began to appear.

Out of the west they came in flocks, flying into the pimento grove for their morning feed. The Maroon boys shot with their backs to the sun. Their bows sang and their arrows flew as fast as their fingers could reach the quivers slung over their shoulders. Although a few of the arrows missed, there were many birds on the ground for the cooking-pots of Mountain Top village.

The boys grinned as they picked up the birds. It had been a good hunt. Even Charlie said so.

"Do you remember when the young warriors went out last year and the year before? Certainly they didn't do as well as we have done," remarked David, with a laugh.

"We can strut about like peacocks when we get back," Uriah said. "The village will be eating our food for some time."

"I shot more birds than anybody else!" Charlie declared, his eyes shining. "I never lost an arrow!"

None of the boys could tell whether this had been so or not. Everybody had been at work together.

"All right, Charlie, we'll tell Chief Phillip so that he will give you more than anybody else," David said.

Charlie's face was troubled. He knew that the Maroons did not like boasters, and that Chief Phillip would find a way to show his displeasure.

"Well, perhaps not more than anybody else," Charlie said in a low voice. Then he brightened. "But I shot many, though."

"So did we all," Uriah said.

"We must start back now," Tommy said. "Let's pick up the birds and go."

The boys began to collect the birds. But Johnny, who had been silent while the other boys were speaking, leaned his head on one side. He seemed to be listening.

"What is it, Johnny?" Tommy asked.

"I don't know," Johnny said. "I just have a queer feeling."

"Do you hear something?"

"I am not quite sure," Johnny repeated. His eyes were half-closed.

Tommy knew that his friend Johnny had a keener sense of sight and hearing than many other boys. This was, perhaps, because he spoke so little.

39

Tommy gave a peculiar whistle and all the boys stood still, for Tommy had given a danger signal. He held up his hand and they waited in silence.

Johnny was turning his head from side to side. Presently, his companions saw him looking hard towards the east. A flight of pigeons suddenly darted from among the trees in that direction and flew off wildly.

Johnny whispered one word, "People."

"Who?" Tommy asked.

"Wait," said Johnny.

Then he seemed to be listening for something on the other side, to the west. This time it was the screech of parakeets that disturbed the silence. They flew up out of the bush, quarrelling as they flapped rapidly away.

"And over there too," said Johnny. "People."

The boys did not ask him whether he was sure. They could see that he was from the look on his face. All the young Maroons suddenly turned to look at Tommy. He was their leader, and now that danger was at hand, they silently appealed to him.

The boys had no doubt that the presence of strange people in the forest meant danger. They also knew that, if these people were Maroons, the birds would not have flown up as they had done. The Maroons were like ghosts when they moved through the forest. They stepped so lightly that no birds could hear them.

"Tommy, what shall we do?" whispered Charlie. He looked frightened.

Tommy was not sure what to do. He had never had enemies in his country. Boys of his age had only heard about the Maroon wars with the Redcoats. But he was bred to battle and to the bush, and so he smiled at Charlie.

"We'll have to do some scouting."

"Scouting? Why don't we run away? We're only boys!

If they are English soldiers, we cannot fight them!" cried Charlie.

"Tommy did not say we should fight them," Uriah said. "He said we should scout them to see who they are."

"Yes, we should scout them," agreed David. He looked at Charlie and said, "Charlie and I will go."

"No! I say we should run away! We should go back at once to Mountain Top and tell them!" said Charlie.

"Tell them what?" asked Tommy. "That we saw some birds fly up out of the bush, and that we ran away from the birds?"

"Tell them it's the English!" cried Charlie.

"And what shall we say when Chief Phillip asks how many were in the mountains, how were they armed, and how many muskets they had? Besides, how do we know that they are Redcoats? Should we lie to Chief Phillip?" Tommy asked angrily.

"Tommy, if we're going to scout them, let us begin now. I think those on our right will be passing through our clearing," Johnny said softly.

"Thank you, Johnny," Tommy said. "All right. David, you and I will scout the east. Johnny and Uriah, you take the other side."

"What about me?" Charlie asked.

"I thought you were running away," Tommy said.

"I cannot go alone," Charlie said.

"Then you'll stay here and wait for us. Hide the birds that we shot. See if there are any arrows lying on the ground. Then take cover until the people have passed. If they are friends, we'll signal to you."

Tommy knew that Charlie would be in no real danger. The Maroons were very clever at hiding in the forest. In any case, it would have been difficult to make them out, dressed as they were in branches and leaves.

Waving to Charlie, the other boys went off. One might

say that they melted into the bush. For that was how it seemed. They just stepped out of the clearing and became a part of the forest.

Tommy and David went east, flitting from tree to tree, walking on the soft, flat part of their feet, just behind the toes. The young Maroons had been trained to walk like this. If they walked on their toes, they might try to grip the ground with them. In doing so they might cause their toes to come in contact with dried twigs or leaves, which might snap noisily. This could result in their capture or death.

After they had gone a short way into a thicket, Tommy and David halted to listen. They heard sounds and looked at each other sharply. The people approaching were certainly not Maroons, for the boys could hear the rattle of arms and the crunch of boots on the ground.

"If they ever depended on hunting for their food they would starve to death," David whispered softly. "They sound like horses."

Tommy shook his head and pointed to the ground. The boys sank to their bellies in the thicket. Carefully, they looked each other over. David saw that the back of Tommy's heel was showing and heaped some more leaves on it. Then they waited, hardly seeming to breathe.

The two young warriors had chosen the thicket because they knew that, if the strangers were soldiers, they would be walking along the clearer parts of the forest. From where Tommy lay, he could look along the ground for some distance without moving his head. He saw the roots of a dogwood tree near to his right hand, and on them a line of ants going up and down. As the ants passed each other, they seemed to stop and whisper before going on again. Tommy knew they were following their trail by scent and only seemed to meet because it was so narrow. If he drew his finger across the trail, it would throw them into confusion until they repaired the scent. Grinning, he rubbed a tiny spot with his finger. He watched the lower trail of ants as they first reached the place. They piled up, not knowing what to do. Then those on the upper side of the root also reached the spot. Some halted. Others went off on both sides. It was just as if they had reached a river on their path and found that the bridge over it was down. Tommy suddenly stopped paying attention to the ants, because the crunch of boots drew nearer.

When he saw the first soldiers, Tommy grew stiff with fright. He did not know they would look like that. True, the Maroon boys had always heard about the Redcoats. Their fathers had drawn pictures in words, and the boys had thought that they would have been able to tell what the English soldiers looked like, although they had never seen any of them. But it was their boots that put the first fears into Tommy. Big, ugly boots, mounted on great pads of leather soles, crushing everything under them! Tommy ran his eyes up the rough blue trousers of the man in front and looked, for the first time, at the scarlet jacket which had given the soldiers the name Redcoats. From where he lay on the ground, he could not see the soldier's face but he saw that the man was carrying a musket.

There were others behind him, all walking slowly. They seemed to be scouts, for they were uncertain of the trail. Tommy almost spoke out in disgust at their clumsy scouting, but a stab of pain in his right hand took his thoughts off the soldiers.

As he gazed at the back of his hand, Tommy froze with horror, for he saw that a couple of the ants had crawled on it. Their trail having been destroyed, they were wandering around.

Tommy felt another jab of pain. Sweat broke out on his face. He dared not move. The Redcoats were still passing. For the next two minutes, Tommy knew the wisdom of the training he had received. For while the ants nibbled away at his flesh, he lay there without sound or movement.

When the last of the soldiers had gone, David looked over at him. He saw the sweat on Tommy's face, and thought that he must have been frightened.

"Were you very frightened?" David whispered. Instead of replying, Tommy showed his hand to David. One of the ants had dropped off but the other was still there, biting. There was a little swelling on the back of the hand.

"No!" gasped David. "Was this happening while the soldiers were passing?"

Tommy nodded. Angrily, David rubbed at the last ant on Tommy's hand. The pain did not linger, and for that Tommy was glad. He grinned sheepishly at David.

"It was my fault," he said, and told David how he had destroyed the ants' trail.

"Did you count how many soldiers there were?" Tommy asked.

David showed his hands twice. That meant twenty. Tommy had counted that number too. They waited for a few minutes to give the soldiers time to walk past Charlie. When they heard Charlie croaking the frog-signal to them, they rose and hurried back to him. Johnny and Uriah were already in the clearing.

"They passed right by me!" Charlie was saying. "I could have touched them, but they were blind!"

"Did you pick up the arrows and everything else on the ground?" Johnny asked.

"Of course. What do you take me for?" said Charlie.

"I hope you did, for I think one of them is suspicious. He's coming back," Johnny said softly.

The boys froze where they were. Tommy was facing Johnny. He saw Johnny looking steadily into the distance behind him. He watched Johnny's eyes, the only part of him which was visible. Johnny saw Tommy watching him and barely moved his head as he nodded to Tommy. Slowly, Tommy turned his whole bush-clad body to prevent it suddenly jerking around and attracting attention.

Tommy could see the Redcoat. The soldier had just entered the clearing on the other side and stood on the edge of the trees. With his musket held in readiness, he looked all around him but, of course, he saw nothing but trees. He could not tell that some of what appeared to be smaller trees were, in fact, Tommy and the other young warriors. Then the soldier glanced at something in his hand. It was an arrow!

The soldier said to himself: "It must be an old arrow. There's nobody here."

If he had been a man of the bush, he would have noticed the fresh scar on the arrow caused by the bowstring when it was released. But he just shrugged his shoulders and turned back to rejoin his companions.

Uriah turned quickly to Charlie.

"So you picked them all up, did you? Would you like to know what we think of you? Do you want to hear?"

Charlie was ashamed.

"I am sorry," he said. "I—I really thought I had picked them up. However, no harm has been done."

"Oh no? You only nearly got us all killed or captured," David said. "I don't know how you were made into a young warrior!"

"Stop that!" Tommy said sharply, for he had seen the pain in Charlie's face. He, and Johnny too, knew that Charlie was having his own secret sufferings. Charlie had cheated, and could never forget that he had cheated.

"All right. Any one of us could make a mistake," Tommy said. "Now, we have work to do. We must get back to Mountain Top as swiftly as we can. We will hold a council. Charlie, have you anything to say?"

Charlie shook his head. Tommy looked at each of the other boys. Uriah spoke when Tommy's eyes rested on him.

"The trouble is, we have these birds and the coneys. It will be hard for us to travel swiftly."

"I know. That is why I'm holding council. What shall we do?" Tommy asked.

"One of us should go," Johnny said.

"Right, Johnny. Only, I would send two, just in case anything happens to one," Tommy said.

"Then you mean the rest of us could come on more slowly, bringing the game?" David asked.

"That's it," Tommy replied. "The birds and coneys will be needed even more in the village, if it is going to be attacked. We *must* take them in."

"I don't see how they can find our village. It's too well hidden," Uriah said.

"They found Nanny Town," Johnny quietly reminded him.

The boys were silent at this reminder. It brought back to their minds one of the saddest events in the history of the Maroons. Nanny Town had been high up in the Blue Mountains, yet the Redcoats had managed to climb the mountain, surprise the villagers, and destroy the village. Since then, villages such as Mountain Top had always sent out their scouts to keep watch.

"And, Tommy, the soldiers whom Uriah and I watched, they had swivel guns. What about the ones you saw?" asked Johnny.

Tommy swallowed and shook his head. Swivel guns! It was swivel guns that had caused so much damage at Nanny Town.

"They will not be able to surprise us at Mountain Top. Our scouts and our sentries are always on the look-out. But, by the time our scouts see them, they will be too near to the village with their swivel guns. We, Johnny and I, can travel many, many times faster than the Redcoats. We'll be at Mountain Top long before our scouts could know the Redcoats are coming," Tommy said.

"You mean, you and Johnny will be going?" Uriah asked. "Why don't you take Charlie instead? Charlie is fastest among us. He won the race to Lookout Rock."

Tommy looked into Charlie's eyes, but Charlie turned his head away.

"Charlie won't mind if I take Johnny. He would prefer to help you bring in the game, for he is stronger than Johnny and can carry a heavier load. Isn't that so, Charlie?" Tommy asked softly.

Charlie nodded his head. "Yes. Yes. I'll help with the load."

David looked surprised. "It's the first time I've heard Charlie agree to do some hard work," he said, shaking his head.

"Never mind that," Tommy said quickly. "Let us be going now. You boys know where the coneys are. Watch out when you're getting to the village. The Redcoats are noisy enough and you shouldn't run into them by mistake. But you never can tell. They may stop to eat or for some other reason. So, walk good."

Tommy and Johnny took off their bows and handed them to the other boys. They removed the quivers which were now again full of the arrows they had taken out of the birds. Now they had only their knives. They gave the Maroon sign, which was the same for both greeting and farewell. People nowadays shake hands when they meet or when they separate, but the Maroons held the palms of their right hands up to shoulder level. The shaking of hands was first practised by the swordsmen of ancient days to show that their hands were free of weapons. The showing of the palms of their hands by the Maroons served the same purpose.

CHAPTER SIX

THE MISSION

Tommy and Johnny had never in their lives run as hard a race as they did that morning. Not even the one to Lookout Rock had been as strenuous. They knew that everything depended on how much time Chief Phillip had before the Redcoats found the village. Perhaps he would have to move the women and children. For, as they ran, Johnny had gasped out some awful news to Tommy. It seemed that the soldiers Tommy had seen had not been the main band. Johnny had counted over a hundred men, and no less than five swivel guns.

It would be a task for the Maroons to move the women and children into the mountains. There were a few old men and women who would have to be carried much of the way. The children, too, would have to be kept in order, for too much noise would betray their movements.

The boys had seen no Maroon scouts, for they had taken a wide circle to avoid meeting any of the Redcoats. Moreover, they were approaching the village from the mountain side. As nobody would expect the Redcoats to come from that end, they met no Maroon sentries either. Tommy stumbled a few times as they neared the village, but he gritted his teeth and ran on. He wished that he was as good at running as Johnny.

Johnny dropped back a little to run with him.

"No—no—!" gasped Tommy. "You go on—hurry! I'll make it!"

He arrived only a short distance behind Johnny. Together they staggered down the village street at high noon. Somebody saw them and shouted. Soon there were more shouts and the boys were lifted off their feet. They were taken into the shade of an ackee tree, where they told their story. A few Maroons ran to inform Chief Phillip of the news. By the time the boys had finished, the abeng was sounding the call of battle. Men came running out from every quarter. It had been years since the abeng had been blown in that fashion, but none of the men had forgotten its signal.

Tommy heard the abeng and tried to stand, but his mother pressed him back.

"Here, son, drink this first," she said firmly.

Tommy smelled the mint tea she was offering him. It had been brewed from the mint-bush that his mother had tended carefully behind the house. The tea was sweetened with cane juice, and Tommy drank it all.

"How do you feel now, son?" his mother asked.

"Much better, mother," he said. "I can really get up now."

"Go to the Council-house. I think that, this time, Chief Phillip will let you in."

His mother was right. The Council-man who kept the door opened it when Tommy came up.

"We were just about to send for you. The Chief wants both you and Johnny."

"I'll call Johnny," Tommy said.

"Johnny's inside. He came along just as you did. How did you know that the Chief wanted to see you? You are smart boys."

"Perhaps there are things we have forgotten," Tommy said. "We may remember them while the Council-men are talking, and tell them to Chief Phillip."

"That's it. Go in, boy. We're all proud of you and the others."

Tommy went in. The roof of the Council-house was very high. Although the light inside was dim, he could see clearly after a while. All the Council-men and some of the chief warriors were gathered in the cool, big room. Tommy knew his father was somewhere in the room but did not search for him. Instead, he looked straight at Chief Phillip.

The Chief was sitting on the Stool of State on a small platform at the end of the room. Made of mahogany, the stool gleamed softly in the dim light. Tommy could remember the history of the Stool. It was shaped like the one his forefathers had known in Africa, the Old Country. He did not know Africa, but, on moonlight nights, he used to hear the old Maroons talking about the Golden Stool of the Ashanti people. In the Old Country, the kings of the Ashanti people were crowned as they sat on the Golden Stool.

Tommy nearly jumped when he saw Johnny sitting on the platform! Johnny was sitting on the floor at Chief Phillip's feet. Suddenly, Tommy heard the Chief calling his name.

"Tommy, come up and sit here with Johnny," Chief Phillip said.

Tommy went as quickly as he could through a row of men seated on mats on the floor. The strong voice of the Chief was still ringing in his ear. It was a stunning thing to hear one's name called out by the Chief in the Council-house. Like one in a dream Tommy reached the platform.

"Sit beside me, Tommy," he heard Johnny say.

Johnny appeared as calm as if he had been sitting on the platform every day of his life.

"Aren't you frightened, Johnny?" asked Tommy in a whisper.

"No," said Johnny. "When we were in the bush I was more afraid."

"It's funny," thought Tommy, "that now I'm afraid and Johnny is not. Yet I'm never afraid in the bush."

Tommy stopped thinking about himself as Chief Phillip spoke.

"Captain Dick, have you tripled the scouts? Have you sent out more sentries?"

"Yes, Chief Phillip," Captain Dick said from the floor. "Wherever we had one scout, there are now three. And the same goes for the sentries. We have placed them in the tallest trees, some of which are as far as five miles from Mountain Top. Our scouts have gone much farther. They are trying to find the Redcoats, and will be sending back messages to us all the time. We'll be able to follow the movements of the Englishmen."

"Good, Captain Dick," Chief Phillip said. "If we must, then we will have everything ready to leave the village. The women must be told to take only what they can carry easily. We may have to move fast."

"Do you think we'll have to leave the village and retreat into the high mountains, Chief?" a Council-man asked.

"I'll tell you what our two young warriors saw. Then you can tell me whether you think we can stay," Chief Phillip replied.

"If we are moving at night, we'll rope the children together to prevent them from being lost," said a Councilman.

All the others agreed. For, several years before, the Maroons, in a retreat before the Redcoats in the parish we now know as Portland, had lost many of their children. They had fallen over the precipices during the night.

"Now, we will talk about the battle," Chief Phillip said. "From what we learn from Tommy and Johnny, there must be about a hundred and twenty Redcoats on the march with, perhaps, six or seven swivel guns. Isn't that so, boys?"

"Yes, sir," said Tommy and Johnny together.

"We have only fifty men in the village. This includes those warriors who are too old to fight and the young warriors," the Chief said.

"We cannot win the battle then," one of the warriors said.

"Our village will be destroyed," said another.

"We must get help," the Chief said.

"But help may come too late to save the village," a third warrior warned.

Voices were raised and many of the Maroons were talking at once. Sometimes, Chief Phillip would point to one of the warriors, and the others would remain still while that warrior spoke. Many plans were discussed; but so far there was full agreement on none.

"Please, sir," said a small voice beside Tommy. Johnny was attempting to speak but the Chief did not hear him.

"Please, Chief Phillip," Johnny said more loudly.

Tommy's eyes opened wide in wonder. What was Johnny doing? Was he going to speak in the Council-house? No boy had ever been allowed to sit in the Council-house before, let alone speaking in it.

"Please, sir!" Johnny said, very loudly now, and tugged at Chief Phillip's foot.

The Chief frowned and looked down at Johnny. Tommy was really frightened now.

"Please, why don't you do to the English as we, young warriors, did to the coneys?" Johnny said.

Chief Phillip held up his hand, and there was silence in the room. The men saw that Chief Phillip was looking down at Johnny and frowning. So they looked at the boy too. Johnny didn't seem to mind.

"What do you mean, boy?" the Chief asked. "How can we treat the English warriors as we treat the coney?"

"Well, sir, last night during the hunt, Tommy was very smart in the way he planned to catch the coneys," Johnny said. "We could use the same plan against the English."

Chief Phillip shook his head. His face was very serious.

"I did not expect that a young warrior would be telling jokes at a time like this," he scolded.

"Please, sir, I am not joking," Johnny said.

At last, Tommy decided that he would speak. He was at first struck dumb by Johnny's boldness but now he had to defend his friend.

"Sir, Johnny never jokes," Tommy said in a loud voice. "Johnny is smarter than almost any other young warrior that I know, sir."

53

Chief Phillip was puzzled. He could not believe that the boys would be so foolish as to joke in the Council-house.

"Very well, Johnny," he said. "Tell me what you mean by doing to the Redcoats as you did to the coneys."

"Well, sir," Johnny said, with more courage now, "last night, we knew we could not allow the coneys to go into their holes. So we stopped the holes with stones. We made the coneys go where we wanted them to go. We made them stay in the open."

"Yes. Yes. We know that, boy. We have hunted the coneys too. But the Redcoats will not be trying to get into holes," Chief Phillip said.

"No, sir. But they will be trying to get into our village. So we should not allow them to get there. We should make them go where we want them to go, just as we did to the coneys."

Tommy suddenly felt pleased, for he could now see what his friend meant.

"Yes, yes, Johnny!" he cried, forgetting his fears. "We could lead them away from the village!"

"And meanwhile, we could send for help, sir," continued Johnny calmly.

Everybody in the big hut looked at the boys. For a moment they could not believe what they had heard. Then a great shout went up. Men jumped to their feet, cheering the two boys; and as he looked down at them, the Chief smiled and shook his head in wonder. Tommy was grinning from ear to ear, but Johnny remained as calm as ever. It was only when his eyes met Tommy's that he smiled slightly.

Chief Phillip waved his hand and the noise stopped.

"My Council-men and warriors," the Chief said, "do you know what we have heard today? We have heard two Maroon boys suggest that we turn the Redcoats into coneys!"

The whole Council burst out into laughter. Tommy could see his father standing up among the warriors, his eyes shining with pride. Even more proud was Johnny's father. The warriors nearest to him were clapping him on his shoulder. Chief Phillip allowed the laughter to go on for a while, and then called for silence.

"All right, Council-men and warriors. Our two young warriors have given us the best plan. With two such as these, the Maroon people will never be defeated. And now, we must make ready."

Chief Phillip looked around the Council-house, his eyes resting on each of his captains in turn.

"We must be prepared. Each captain must see that his men are ready," the Chief ordered. Then he continued in a lower voice: "Some of us may die. Maroons have never been afraid of dying. But we will never be dishonoured. Swear by your swords!"

The Council-house seemed to shake with the roar that rose from the men. There was a *clank* as swords were drawn and raised in the air.

"By the sword of the Maroons!" the warriors shouted.

Then they were marching from the hut, singing a Maroon song. Tommy and Johnny too were swept outside in the rush.

Full of excitement, the boys watched the preparations of the warriors. The great war quivers were swiftly filled with arrows, and muskets were cleaned until they shone. Around some large fires in the village street women were cooking food for the warriors to take with them. In one corner, over another fire, a few warriors were making bullets from lead captured in old raids on English settlements.

Tommy watched as the warriors put the lead into pots to boil. Using a clay mould, they dipped the boiling lead out of the pot. They then held the mould in a pot of cold water until the lead cooled in the shape of a bullet. The bullets were afterwards dropped on cocoa leaves and left to harden.

Most of the men had muskets, but a few would depend on their bows. The Maroon bowmen were very famous. They would go close to the enemy and shoot from the trees in the gullies. Almost every Maroon was a marksman. They were equally good with bow or musket.

One of the warriors making the bullets was an old man. He was humming a song to himself as he worked. He looked up when he heard Tommy approaching.

"Hello, Tommy, the great young warrior," he said with a smile. "Have you ever fired a musket?"

"No," Tommy said. "But I would like to."

"Oh, you will," said the old warrior. "We'll have to get a musket for you very soon. Boys like you and Johnny and the other young warriors are worthy of muskets."

"Especially Johnny. It was he who thought of the plan," Tommy said. "Have you ever fired a musket in war?"

The old warrior nodded his head as he worked.

"Many times, boy," he said. "My band used to live up in the Blue Mountains, in the place the English now call St. Thomas-in-the-East. I was at a town, near the Cockpits."

"You have been all over Jamaica!" cried Tommy.

"Yes. Most of my friends are dead now, some of them killed by Redcoat bullets. But we are still fighting, boy. We'll never surrender."

"Have you ever been afraid in battle?"

"Oh, yes. But the thing to do is to fight on, even when you are afraid," said the old man. "Soon the fear will grow ashamed of itself and go away."

"Tell me about one of those times when you were afraid," Tommy said.

"It was at the Battle of Nanny Town," the old warrior

said. "The English swivel guns had smashed our village and it was night and I was lying alone in a gully."

"Why were you alone? Where were the others?"

The old man smiled sadly. "That was a dreadful day, my son. I hope you will never know one like it in your own life. Many of our people had been killed by the enemy's swivel guns, large guns fired by three or four men and loaded with shots as big as your head. The English soldiers turned them from side to side as they fired them. I was alone because those who had not been killed by the English guns had leaped over deep precipices to their deaths. They preferred death to capture. The others had taken the women and children and gone to join another band..."

"Why didn't you go with them?"

"I was wounded," the old man said. "An English bullet had caught me, and I lay in the gully during the night unable to move. All around me I could hear the Redcoats searching for any Maroons who were left behind."

"They beat us that time," Tommy said.

"Yes. This was the first time they had ever beaten us. They have never been able to do so again."

"We have won many times since," Tommy said.

"And we will win again, son. They have more and better guns than we have. But we know the country better and can move more quickly. We are the Old Jamaicans. The mountains belong to us."

"But why were you afraid then, even more than you were during the battle?"

"It is when you are helpless that you are most fearful," the old man said. "If I could have stood and fought, perhaps I would not have been afraid. But as I lay in the dark and watched the torches of the Englishmen coming nearer and nearer, I was afraid. For I did not want to die lying on my back, helpless before the Redcoat."

"What did you do?"

The old warrior laughed softly as he took up more lead in the earthenware mould.

"What did I do, boy? I crawled. For a whole night and a day, I crawled. And I crawled for another night and another day, until my people found me."

The old man laughed again and said: "A few minutes ago you said that I knew Jamaica. Oh, yes, I know it more than most people. For two nights and two days my face was never more than an inch from the Jamaican earth. I saw every ant, every worm, every blade of grass for miles and miles. Whenever I wanted to rest I just let my chin drop to the ground."

Tommy shook his head, thanked the old man for sparing him some time and went to look for Johnny.

He was going down the street to Johnny's place when he heard his name being called. He turned back and saw a warrior behind him.

"Tommy," he said, "the Chief wants you at the Council-house. You and Johnny."

"Johnny? I'm looking for him now," said Tommy.

"I'll find him. You go to the Chief," he said.

By the time Tommy reached the Council-house, Johnny had overtaken him. They looked at each other wonderingly as they went in. They could not even guess why Chief Phillip had summoned them.

This time, only the Council-men were with Chief Phillip. They all sat on beautiful straw mats made from silver thatch and spread on the ground. The boys went and stood beside Chief Phillip.

"Now, Tommy and Johnny," the Chief said, "would you be afraid to go again into the forest?"

"No, sir!" the boys cried together.

"We need help from our brother Maroons, but I can't afford to send any of the men to seek it. We must have every warrior here. Will you boys go? Your task will be a very dangerous one."

"We will, sir," the boys said.

"As soon as we begin to fight the enemy, they will be on their guard more than ever. It will take much bravery and much cleverness to get past them," Chief Phillip said.

"Where will you be sending us, sir?" Tommy asked.

"There's another band of Maroons in the mountains to the west," Chief Phillip said. "You will march due west."

Chief Phillip went on to tell the boys of the rivers they would cross, and of the valleys in which they had to be very careful. Chief Phillip said the Redcoats liked to camp in the valleys. There were also sugar cane estates in the valleys, where there would be soldiers.

Then Chief Phillip held up his hand. The warrior who blew the abeng, stepped forward.

"When you have entered the mountains, after crossing the valley, you will be in the country of the Maroons. But you may never find them unless you call them," Chief Phillip said. "And so, we will teach you how to use the abeng to make the call which will bring our friends to you. Then you will tell them I sent you for help. They are the Mocho Maroons and their chief is Chief James."

And so it was that, later that day, when Charlie, David and Uriah at last came into the village with the game, they were surprised to see Tommy and Johnny learning to blow the abeng. They laughed at the way Tommy and Johnny looked as they tried to blow the horn. With their jaws puffed up they looked just like two little pigs. But in the end they learnt to make the call for help. The sound they made began with a long, low moan, which became higher and higher, went down again, and then died away. Charlie, David and Uriah looked on, wishing that they were as lucky as Tommy and Johnny.

The other three young warriors had their moment of

triumph, however. The village welcomed them as heroes, for the meat that they had brought was worth much to a people preparing for war.

By nightfall, the village was on a war footing. All muskets had been cleaned. The shotbags of the warriors were full of leaden bullets. Swords and cutlasses were sharpened. The musket-men had their powder-horns filled. Everything that the women could carry had been packed. Chief Phillip hoped that he would not have to move the women and children. Yet, like a wise leader, he was fully prepared.

News had come in earlier that the scouts had found the enemy, who, of course, did not know that they had been seen. Every move they made from then on would be carefully observed and reported to the Maroon Chief.

Late that evening a warrior went for Tommy and Johnny and took them to Captain Dick, a short, strong man with broad shoulders. He was the War Captain, the man who would lead the Maroons into battle.

"We have just had some bad news from the scouts," Captain Dick said. "The Redcoats are spread too widely in the mountains for us to send out you two boys alone."

"We can get through, Captain Dick!" cried Tommy.

Captain Dick smiled. "We can't take the chance, Tommy. You may be caught and then we would never get the help we need."

"Do you mean we won't be allowed to go?" asked Johnny.

They waited breathlessly for his answer.

"You will go," Captain Dick said at last. "But we will take you through the English line."

"Take us through the line?"

"Yes. Now, go and get ready. When the abeng blows, we will be ready to march out." Then Captain Dick added, laughing, "We will be ready to play the coney game, the one Johnny told us about."

The boys went to their homes. Tommy found his father waiting. He was wearing his powder-horn and shotbag, and a shining cutlass hung at his side. He had a musket in his hand, and his face was very serious. It was the first time that Tommy had seen him dressed for war.

Tommy's mother held her hands out to her son and he went to her.

"I know, my son," she said, putting her arms around him, "that you are just as ready to go as your father is."

Tommy looked up at his father. He noticed the leather band he had around his forehead, and knew that it was there to hold leaves and branches during an ambush. The Maroons always fought by ambush, as they were too small in number to fight in any other way. They would lead the enemy into a place where they could trap them.

"Has Captain Dick spoken to you, son?" his father asked.

Tommy said: "Yes, father. Will you be going too?"

"I will be with the warriors going north. You will be going west. Don't be afraid. Captain Dick will be with you. Now, come to me."

"I'm not afraid, father. But I wish you were going with us," Tommy said going across the room to his father.

"Tommy," said his father, "for a boy who has just been made a young warrior you have been greatly honoured. But remember that how you act in this will mean a great deal to the Maroon people, not only us in Mountain Top but other Maroons as well."

"In years to come, our story-tellers will tell their tales of you and Johnny," his mother said softly, "there will be other children sitting in the moonlight and listening to the tales of two brave young warriors named Tommy and Johnny. So, tonight, you must be brave, my son."

"He will be brave," his father said, resting his hand on Tommy's shoulder. "When you have said good-bye to your mother, come over to the shot-maker's fire. We must prepare you."

After leaving his mother, Tommy hurried to the shot-maker's fire. He was eager to know how they would prepare him. Johnny was already there, with his father. The old warrior who made the shots was also there with an earthenware jar in his hand. Both boys were stripped to the waist. Their fathers then took some of the pleasant-smelling ointment from the jars and rubbed it all over them.

"It is made from herbs," the old warrior told them. "It will make you smell like the forest, and so it will be very difficult for the Redcoats to find you."

The boys already knew about the ointment, for they had seen scouts using it. It made their skins so slippery that they could easily escape from any Redcoat who tried to hold them.

Tommy and Johnny met Charlie, Uriah and David as they walked to the meeting-place of the warriors. In the light of the camp fires, the other boys stared in amazement at Tommy and Johnny.

"You have put on the ointment of herbs!" Uriah whispered. "You are warriors!"

Tommy and Johnny grinned. They were not yet warriors but they were proud that they had been called upon to serve as warriors.

"You are going all the same? We heard that the Redcoats were too many for anybody to get past them," Charlie said in a voice that showed how envious he was.

"Yes. Captain Dick will go a part of the way with us," Tommy said.

"They should have sent me. I am the oldest and I could go more quickly," Charlie said.

"You have a way of not being careful enough when the Redcoats are around. Don't you remember the arrow you left on the ground for the Redcoats to pick up?" asked David.

The other boys smiled.

"I hope that after the Redcoats have caught and hanged you, Chief Phillip will send me," Charlie said angrily to Tommy, who was standing close to him.

"But this time I hope you will not turn back before you have finished the journey, as you did on the run to Lookout Rock," Tommy said, so softly that only Charlie heard him.

Charlie's jaw dropped in surprise, and the shame showed plainly in his eyes. He did not know that anybody had seen him when he had cheated on the run to Lookout Rock.

Tommy walked quickly away with Johnny. He was sorry he had hurt Charlie, but, perhaps, it was better that Charlie should know he was not fooling everyone. It might help him to mend his ways.

CHAPTER SEVEN

THROUGH ENEMY LINES

THE moon had not yet risen when the Maroon war party left the village. Silent as shadows, they disappeared swiftly into the dark forest. They moved so rapidly that often Tommy and Johnny had to trot to keep up with them.

Captain Dick's party, with whom the boys travelled, was to lure the Redcoats out of their lines so Tommy and

Johnny could slip through. The Captain had told them that he hoped to be at the English line just before daylight.

"That is the time when people sleep heaviest," Captain Dick told them. "Never attack an enemy camp in the dead of night, for the guards are very much awake then. Attack when dawn is near. They always think that all danger is past by then."

The Maroons went more cautiously as they drew near to the spot where their first scout had been posted. Every now and then they halted, and Captain Dick hooted like an owl. He would hoot three times, pause, and then hoot again a fourth time. After a while the party got an answering hoot and they halted.

Neither of the boys saw when one of the Maroon scouts came up. They only heard a whispered conversation, and the line of men moved forward once again. Tommy tried to see the scout as he went, but all he saw was a dark bulk of trees. Yet perhaps one of those trees was the scout himself.

The rising moon was just lighting the tops of the trees when the party stopped again. Tommy could make out about twenty Maroons travelling with Captain Dick. He knew his father had gone with another band, but he had been hoping to see him all the same. Neither did Johnny's father seem to be in the party. This time, when the owl-hoot was heard, Tommy saw the scout who came up. He was a warrior named Peter, who had made a famous name for himself as a scout.

Peter's shoulder glistened in the moonlight and Tommy knew that he too had been rubbed with ointment. The scout walked so lightly as he crossed the clearing towards them, that his feet hardly seemed to touch the ground.

"How is the night?" Captain Dick asked as Peter came up.

"Peaceful," Peter said.

"And the enemy?"

"Except for their scouts, they sleep," Peter said.

"I do not want to meet their scouts," Captain Dick said.

"I will take you to the place which I have cleared for you."

"Have you done so already?" Captain Dick asked.

"My comrade and I removed three English scouts. Now the way is open."

"Who is your comrade?"

"Scout Jim."

In the moonlight, Tommy looked at Johnny. Of course, the boys knew Scout Jim too. He and Peter were the most famous of the Maroon scouts. From what had been said the boys gathered that the two Maroons must have stolen upon the Redcoats' camp and killed their scouts.

"All right, we're ready," Captain Dick said. Then he spoke to the boys: "We're near to the English camp. You will stay by me. But you must be so quiet that not even I will feel that you are near."

And so through the night went the Maroons once more. They appeared as dark, shadowy figures. Never walking along a straight path they darted from tree to tree, the light of the moon hardly ever touching them. Tommy and Johnny watched Captain Dick and tried to follow him closely in everything he did. This was not too difficult, for they had been used to the forest from the time they could walk and could therefore move noiselessly.

A little before dawn, Captain Dick and his men reached the edge of a low ridge that overlooked the Redcoats' camp. They were now in a position to attack. The bush around them was not very high; but high enough to conceal them. They crouched and waited.

As soon as the first flush of day appeared on the distant peaks, Captain Dick turned to the boys. There was determination in his face.

"Do you remember what I told you?" he asked the two young warriors.

"Yes, Captain Dick," they answered.

"Repeat it to me, Tommy."

"We must wait until the Redcoats have followed you out of sight. Then we must be away before they return."

"And suppose you are captured?" Captain Dick asked.

"We must not say that we have been sent to seek help but that we are only out hunting," Tommy said.

"Good. Now be ready. And whatever we do, you must not show yourselves until the Redcoats have followed us."

"Yes, sir."

"Good luck," Captain Dick said, as he turned away.

Taking off his powder horn, Captain Dick carefully measured out some gunpowder. He put a bullet and some powder into the musket and rammed them down into the barrel. Then he looked up at the sky, watching for the first good light. All the other warriors had loaded their muskets too, and they were looking at Captain Dick.

Peering through the weeds, the boys could now see fairly well into the English camp. Around a small fire there was a group of soldiers sleeping on the ground. Wrapped in their cloaks, they had gone to sleep, leaving their scouts to watch. They did not know that the scouts had been killed by Peter and Jim.

Suddenly Tommy felt a touch on his shoulder. He turned and saw Johnny pointing to the right. He looked and saw that Captain Dick was preparing to fire.

The Maroon warrior had rested his musket on a small branch. With his cheek on the barrel and with one eye closed, he carefully pulled the trigger. There was a flash of fire and a loud explosion.

Then Captain Dick sprang to his feet and gave a Maroon yell.

As if they had been pulled by a string, all the English

soldiers suddenly sat up. Some sprang to their feet, staring wildly around. As Captain Dick yelled a second time, they swung in his direction. The Maroon captain waved his musket and shouted. Then he stooped swiftly behind the broom weed. He ran off northwards along the ridge, loading his musket as he went.

A second Maroon took aim and fired. As one of the Redcoats fell, the Maroon sprang upright, waved his musket and yelled. Down he went again, and ran off as Captain Dick had done. Then, one by one, all the Maroons repeated this manœuvre. Now Tommy could see why Captain Dick had chosen this place for the attack. They could shoot, then show themselves before running off. In this way, they hoped that the Redcoats would follow them. And the Redcoats did.

Hurriedly grabbing their weapons, they set off with angry yells after the Maroons. There was a burst of gunfire from both sides. Tommy and Johnny trembled with excitement. They saw that the camp was empty. With a quick look at each other, they began to run for their lives. They raced down the ridge and reached the valley. They ran on, leaping over small stones, trying to be out of the place before the Redcoats returned.

The packs belonging to the English soldiers still lay around the fire. All they had taken with them, when they chased the Maroons, were their muskets. Not knowing when one or two of the soldiers would return to guard the camp, the boys kept looking back as they ran.

While they had been hiding on the ridge, the valley had seemed quite narrow. But now it appeared wider than any other valley they had ever seen. They were hardly halfway across and their hearts were already pounding with the effort. Their breathing was rapid, their legs felt tired and heavy. Yet, if they could have seen themselves running, they would have realised that they were just skimming along. With their greased shoulders shining in the morning light and wearing only their pantaloons, they looked like two small animals running hard to escape their pursuers.

A Redcoat was returning to camp. He stopped, as he saw them, looked, rubbed his eyes and looked again.

"Halt!" he shouted, firing his musket.

But Tommy and Johnny were too far away to be hit, and kept on running.

"A Redcoat!" panted Johnny.

With a quick glance over his shoulder, Tommy saw the soldier.

"Keep running, Johnny! We'll soon be among the trees!" he yelled.

Lowering their heads, the boys ran on. They reached the other side of the valley, scrambled up the ridge and soon were among the trees. They knew it would be dangerous to stop, for the Redcoat might be after them. So, weary as they were, they kept going. The boys felt that they would be safer once they were in the heart of the forest.

They slowed to a trot as soon as they got among the trees. They kept their backs to the sun so that they would be sure that they were travelling west. In this way, they had no fear of losing their way, for Chief Phillip had told them clearly how to reach the Mocho Maroons. They would have to cross rivers and climb cliffs; but the boys knew that they could do it. After all, they had lived all their lives in the mountains.

From time to time, Johnny, his hearing as keen as ever, would stop to listen and Tommy would wait. Johnny looked puzzled, but he shook his head when Tommy questioned him, and they went on.

A little farther on Johnny called a halt, stooped and placed his ear to the ground. Tommy was worried because he had never seen his friend so uncertain before.

"Let us wait and see whether we are being followed," said Tommy.

"If we are, it is not by a Redcoat. Only a Maroon could be so quiet, and if it's a Maroon, then he is a friend," said Johnny.

The sun was high when they stopped. Tommy seemed uneasy. They chose what looked like a good place to eat and rest. The bush grew thick and there was an opening into which they could crawl.

As Johnny stooped to enter the opening, he sniffed. Then he jumped back, pulling Tommy with him.

"A wild boar is in there!" he whispered.

"A—boar!" gasped Tommy.

Swiftly they spun around, looking for a tree. They leaped for the lower branches of one, and they were not a moment too soon. From the bush came a sudden snort. Then there was a loud squeal and a rush of air as a boar charged into the open. Its little eyes gleamed as it rushed forward, snorting and squealing. Then it stopped and put its snout in the air, trying to find the boys' scent. Its tusks were pointed, its hooves were as sharp as knives and dug into the earth, cutting deep lines in it. Tommy trembled as he looked at the savage animal.

Hugging the tree tightly, the two boys watched the fierce animal below them. They knew that the boar depended on its sense of smell rather than its sight. Since the wind was blowing away from them, they hoped that it would not pick up their scent and would soon return to its hole. But they had moved so quickly that they hadn't enough time to choose the best tree. The trunk of the one they occupied was too stout for easy climbing, and the branch to which they clung was very slender. If it broke, they would be flung to the ground.

Had they been armed with their bows, they could have tried shooting the wild boar. But their bows were on the ground. The boys had dropped them when they ran towards the tree. Their arms were growing tired, and the boar showed no intention of leaving. It was still snorting and shaking its head.

"I cannot hold on much longer!" whispered Johnny. "My arms are tiring!"

"Mine too!" gasped Tommy. "But we must not let go!"

"My fingers are numb!" said Johnny.

"If you let go, I will too!" said Tommy. "We will have to run—or fight him with our knives!"

Both boys knew that they could not kill the savage boar with their knives. Their only hope lay in running, and, if they once stumbled, that would be the end of them.

"Wait—!" whispered Johnny. "I hear something!"

It was the little pigs which the boar had left in the den. Frightened at being left alone, they were crying and scratching around. Grunting angrily, the boar whirled around and rushed back into the lair. In an instant the boys dropped from the tree, grabbed their bows and raced away as fast as they could.

They found a safer hiding-place in a pine thicket farther on. This time, they shot a couple of arrows into the thicket before going too close to it. Hearing no grunts, they went in and recovered their arrows.

It was cool and restful inside the thicket. The pine needles on the ground made a soft bed for the weary boys who were tempted to sleep, but knowing that so much depended on them, they decided to sit and rest for a little while. They then ate some of their provisions and drank some water from Tommy's special bottle.

The boys were too tired to keep to their decision. Soon their eyelids drooped and they drifted into a doze.

Johnny suddenly awoke, but did not know why. He only knew that his eyes were open and that he was afraid. Tommy was still asleep, and Johnny touched him softly.

Tommy woke with a start but Johnny held up a warning finger. Putting his mouth close to Tommy's ear, he whispered, "People are coming." Quickly Tommy sat up. He could hear cautious footsteps approaching.

"Are these the footsteps you thought you heard sometime ago?" Tommy asked.

"No. These are too noisy. These people are wearing boots," Johnny said.

On their bellies the boys wriggled to the edge of the thicket. They peered in the direction of the sounds.

Two Redcoats walked into view.

They did not seem to be tracking the boys for they were not watching the ground. Instead, they looked all around them and talked in low voices. Hoping to take another path which would lead them away from the soldiers, the boys waited for them to pass.

But Tommy and Johnny received a cruel surprise; for the Redcoats stopped in the clearing just opposite their hiding-place!

CHAPTER EIGHT

THE COMING OF CHARLIE

THE young Maroons stared at each other. Here they were, like two coneys, caught in their holes. For, although the Redcoats had not seen them, they had stopped just outside the entrance to their hiding-place. The two soldiers sat down wearily, leaning their backs against a tall cedar tree.

"Oh, I feel like a tired racehorse!" said one.

"I don't know how these Maroons can go so quickly through the bush. Every time I walk, a vine or a stone holds me back," said the other.

"I don't think you saw any Maroon boys at all," the first one said. "You saw a pair of goats, or calves, and thought you had seen two boys."

"I tell you I saw them. Plain as I see you now."

Tommy and Johnny were too frightened to move. The soldiers were talking about them.

One of the soldiers was the man who had fired his musket at them in the valley. Tommy decided to take a closer look at them. Quietly as a mouse coming up out of its hole, he parted the bush. He found he could look straight into the men's faces!

The boy remained still as a stone, knowing that if he made no move, the soldiers would hardly see him. One of them was red-haired and tall. The other was short and fat and had a cast in one eye. They had taken off their hats and belts and had placed them on the ground beside their muskets. Tommy turned his head and beckoned to Johnny. A plan was already forming in Tommy's mind although he hoped he would not have to use it.

"How far do you think we have come?" said the tall soldier to his companion.

"I don't know, but it's already too far," replied the other. "I would not like to be lost in this forest."

"The Captain ordered us to hunt for those boys and bring them back. He thinks a Maroon village is somewhere around here and they could lead us to it."

"I would like to drag them back by their heels," said the tall one angrily, "but we can't even find a trace of them."

"All these Maroons are like cats. They leave no trail when they walk through the woods."

"And they are so clever at hiding that they could be anywhere without being seen. They could even be right around here," said the tall one, looking around. "We should have more men so we could make a better search."

The boys trembled as the soldier's eyes swept over their hiding-place. For a moment, he seemed to be looking straight at them.

"Just look at that sun," said the fat one, as he lay on his back and looked through the trees. "Even here, it's hot."

"Don't get too comfortable. You may go to sleep."

The sun had really warmed the forest. Tommy could now smell the pine needles. The smell was becoming stronger as the day grew warmer. He hoped it would not make them sneeze.

Just then, he felt Johnny clutch his arm. Tommy turned quickly. Johnny had one hand clamped over his nose and his eyes were watering. Tommy instantly knew what was wrong. Johnny wanted to sneeze.

Tommy's eyes and mouth opened wide.

"Try not to sneeze," he whispered anxiously.

Luckily, Johnny managed to control himself. The tears left his eyes and he took his hand from his nose and mouth.

"I hope it won't come back," Tommy said.

"I'll try to keep it in if it does," Johnny remarked. "But I have never been able to stand the smell of pines without wanting to sneeze."

"Why didn't you tell me that before?" Tommy remarked.

"I forgot," whispered Johnny.

"We have to get out of here."

"Yes. But how?"

Tommy told him what he had been thinking and planning.

"To crawl to the other side and run?" Johnny said, after he had listened. "But they might see us and shoot us. Then we would never be able to get help for Chief Phillip."

"I know," Tommy said sadly. "But it's our only chance, especially now that you might want to sneeze again. You see, their belts and muskets are on the ground. If we run some distance before they see us, it will take time for them to pick up their muskets, aim and fire."

"Wait, listen to what they are saying."

The fat soldier was speaking, ". . . I think we had better get back. I am hungry."

"There are many fruits in the forest. If you're hungry, pick a fruit from one of the trees."

"Fruit!" said the fat man in disgust. "I want meat. I am too hungry to eat fruit. If only we could find a fat pigeon or coney."

"Yes. Then you would shoot off your musket and bring the Maroons down on us."

"Shoot off my musket?" The fat soldier laughed. "You don't know anything about the Jamaican forests. You have

74

just come out from England. You don't shoot at coneys. You knock them over with stones. I have knocked over even pigeons with stones."

"I am not very good at throwing stones," the other one said. "I think I'll look for a fruit."

He stood up, stretched and pointed to a tree some distance away.

"What's that over there?"

The fat one raised himself on one elbow and looked.

"That? That's a custard apple tree. Very nice. But not for me. I want meat."

"That's why you are so fat," said the tall, thin one. He strode away.

Johnny's eyes were shining. "Now, if we could only get the other one to leave the muskets," he whispered.

"He will leave only for a pigeon or a coney, although I feel like one just now."

"Tommy!" whispered Johnny, "That's it! I'll be the pigeon!"

Johnny pursed his mouth and turned his face upward. Then twice from his throat came the coo-coo-coo-ooo of a pigeon. Tommy put his eye again to the hole through which they were spying on the soldiers. The fat one was sitting upright, turning his head from side to side in an effort to locate the pigeon.

"Listen, do you hear anything?" he called to the other soldier. "That's a pigeon cooing."

He got to his feet quickly and searched the ground for stones. He found a handful and trotted away into the bushes.

"I'll bring back a nice fat one for our supper," he called as he disappeared into the forest.

Glancing at each other, the young warriors scrambled out of their shelter and raced towards the muskets. Before they had covered half the distance, there was a shout and the noise of running feet. Heads down, the boys sprinted for the muskets. They picked up the weapons but they had not guessed how close the tall soldier was. Shouting, he snatched at the boys. His hands closed on Tommy but he could get no grip. The boy's skin was too slippery with the ointment the old warrior had rubbed on it. Yet, the Redcoat managed to delay them, for Johnny would not leave without Tommy.

Just then, the other soldier came into view. The shouts from his companion had alarmed him. When he saw what was happening, he rushed towards the boys with a roar of anger.

Tommy and Johnny were almost in despair. They knew that they could not hope to get away from both Redcoats. They feared both of them might be caught, and then there would be nobody to take the message to Chief James. If that happened, the village of Mountain Top would soon fare as badly as Nanny Town.

Suddenly they saw a sight they could hardly believe. Charlie had entered the clearing!

CHAPTER NINE

A NARROW ESCAPE

SHRIEKING a Maroon war cry, Charlie ran into the clearing straight into the fat soldier's path. The Redcoat grabbed him.

But Charlie clung to the soldier and they began to struggle.

"Run, Tommy, run!" yelled Charlie in a voice that sounded very nearly like crying.

Charlie's shout had attracted the tall soldier's attention. Johnny took the chance to swing the heavy musket at his ankle. There was a sharp crack and the soldier yelped and dropped to the ground. Holding his ankle, he rolled over and over, bawling loudly. Tommy and Johnny escaped.

They ran until they felt as though their chests would burst. After a while, they stopped only long enough to hide the heavy muskets under some dried leaves. They were sure that they would remember the hiding-place. A mahogany tree which had been burnt by lightning marked the spot.

They were staggering by the time they reached the river. Weak and tired, they threw themselves on the bank and lay still until they caught their breath. Then they dragged themselves to the water's edge and drank their fill.

"I—I think we got away from them!" gasped Johnny.

"Not even a swallow could have followed us at the speed at which we ran," Tommy replied.

He sat up and looked at Johnny. "But now we have no food, no bow and no arrows. Only our knives and the abeng. In our haste we have left everything else behind."

"We can't be very far from where we are going," Johnny said.

"No, for now we have reached the river, and we have only the cliff to climb."

Suddenly they stopped talking and stared at each other. They were both thinking of Charlie.

"Charlie!" gasped Tommy. "Where did he come from?"

"He must have been the one I heard following us!" Johnny said. "I knew it had to be a Maroon."

"The Redcoats will kill him!" cried Tommy.

Johnny looked thoughtful.

"No, not if he tells them where our village is," Johnny said, "and promises to take them to it."

"But—but he cannot do that! He's a young warrior!"

"Suppose they torture him?" asked Johnny.

"And I don't think Charlie is very brave."

"Yet, he was brave a while ago," Johnny said.

They looked at each other, not knowing what next to say.

After a moment Tommy spoke. "Why did he do it? Did you hear him? He cried, 'Run, Tommy, run!' Why did he do it?"

"Perhaps because he remembered that he was a Maroon, that he was a young warrior," Johnny said. "Perhaps it was his way of showing he was sorry that he had cheated on the run to Lookout Rock."

Tommy then told Johnny how he had made Charlie know that they had witnessed his trickery.

"He must have been very ashamed," said Johnny softly.

"I am too," said Tommy. "I am ashamed of the way I treated him."

"One has to tell the truth even if it hurts," Johnny said wisely.

Tommy took a deep breath and stared at the water.

"We must rescue him. Even if they torture him and he tells them the way to the village, we must rescue him," he said.

"Yes, I agree. If the village is saved, Charlie will have helped to do it," Johnny said.

"First we must find Chief James because the safety of our people depends on it. Let us cross the river," Tommy said.

The river was not very wide, but it was deep enough for swimming. It had been named the Rio Minho by the Spaniards. In the old days before the English came, the ancestors of Tommy and Johnny had worked on sugar estates on the banks of the Minho.

The boys used their knives to cut poles from among the small trees growing near the river. These they lashed together by stout river rushes. Then they went up along the river bank, found where the water was smoothest and, launching their raft of river rushes, began paddling across the water.

They went as quietly as they could, because crocodiles lived in the river. They knew that the rivers on the south contained the big reptiles, but that those on the northern slopes of the mountain had none. So they kept a sharp look-out as they paddled their raft across.

Downstream on the bank below them, Johnny had his eyes fixed on what looked like a log; but when it suddenly came to life and slipped into the water he shouted, "Tommy, a crocodile!"

No longer did the two boys feel tired. They splashed

and paddled as hard as they could, since the noise did not matter any more. And now they were nearing the bank. But, as Tommy glanced behind him, he could see the reptile speeding through the water. The raft was so flat that by a whisk of its tail, the crocodile could throw the boys into the river.

"Paddle! It is getting closer!" yelled Tommy.

They were out of the deep water now, for they could feel the river's muddy bottom.

"Run! Leave the raft and run!" cried Tommy.

The boys scrambled up the soft, sloping bank of the river until they reached the bush that grew at the water's edge. They dragged themselves out of the water, and heard a splash behind them, as the crocodile went past. Rolling over on the bank, they lay there, panting. It had been a narrow escape!

CHAPTER TEN

CLIMBING THE CLIFF

The young warriors could not stop for a long rest because they knew how much Chief Phillip was depending on them.

It was now quite late in the day for the sun was low in the west. In the distance, the boys saw the cliff which Chief Phillip had urged them to reach before dark. He had warned that they would not be able to climb it by night.

"Is there no other way to get into those mountains?" asked Johnny. "That cliff's going to be hard to climb."

"Chief Phillip said that if we went any other way, we might meet soldiers," Tommy reminded him.

"I would like to meet a few soldiers now," Johnny said.

"Why?" Tommy asked in surprise.

"So that I could get some of their dinner."

The boys laughed—the first time they had since the night before. Charlie's capture by the Redcoats had saddened them. They picked a few star apples and cashew fruits which they found after leaving the river, and hurried on. Tommy shook the water out of the abeng as they walked through grass that was often taller than they.

After a while they entered a grove of guava trees. The wind was whistling among the leaves. Above the sound of the wind, they heard a far-away booming. It grew stronger as they neared the cliff and was soon dinning in their ears. They halted and looked fearfully at each other.

What was it? What new danger was threatening them?

Then Tommy remembered. He grinned and shouted to Johnny. "It's the Talking Rock, the one Chief Phillip told us about. It is the wind that blows through the holes in the cliff and makes that noise."

Johnny laughed and said, "A fine pair of young warriors we are. We run away even from the wind."

"The Chief said that when we got close to the cliff the noise would cease," Tommy remarked.

And true it was; for by the time they were at the foot of the cliff, the booming had stopped. They could see the three great holes in the face of the cliff. The story-tellers among the Maroons said that three rivers had once flowed through these holes. It was said that the stories had come down from the Arawak Indians to the ancestors of the Maroons.

As the Chief had said, the boys found creepers growing at the foot of the cliff. The withes were thick and long and coiled like huge snakes.

"We haven't much daylight left," Tommy said.

"We must hurry then," Johnny urged.

They took out their knives and started to cut the creepers so as to plait them into ropes. They were going to use the ropes to climb the cliff.

"They say the Arawak Indians used to live on top of this cliff," remarked Johnny, gazing upward.

"I wonder what the Arawaks looked like?" said Tommy.

"We'll never know, for now they are all dead."

The young warriors worked as they talked and the ropes were soon ready.

The face of the cliff was very rough, so the boys had little trouble finding places over which they could cast their rope.

Long practice had made the Maroon boys good at casting. In Jamaica there were still wild cattle, the offspring of those left in the forests by the Spaniards who had fled from the country in 1655. Now, almost eighty years later, cattle-hunting was still practised. Often the cattle were shot. But when the Maroons had no gunpowder to spare, they would catch them by throwing ropes around their necks. Like all other Maroon boys, Tommy and Johnny had been taught how to do this.

"Look at that long piece of rock sticking out like a needle," said Johnny, pointing to it. "If we could cast that, we would be half-way up the cliff."

"Yes, but then we would be stuck there," Tommy said. "We must find a ledge, get to it, and then throw to the next one."

After a short search, the boys found what they wanted. Johnny threw first, and missed. The strong wind made it difficult to aim. Tommy also tried, but missed. Then Johnny waited until the wind dropped for a few seconds, and threw. The noose sailed up, seemed to hesitate, then settled over the piece of rock. They tried its strength by tugging at it. It held firmly.

Gripping the vine in their hands and using their toes on the face of the cliff, they climbed up, Tommy ahead. The ascent was difficult and sometimes, when the wind blew hard, they were thrown against the cliff. They were quite breathless by the time they reached the ledge.

Looking back at the way they had taken, they could see the river shining in the distance. But there was no time to lose. The day was ending and the ledge on which they stood was very narrow. They had to find another piece of rock over which to throw their rope. If they waited much longer, they would not be able to see; and one wrong step would send them tumbling down the cliff. This could mean serious injury or even death, for it was a long way to the bottom.

"We must move now," Tommy said. His arms and legs ached.

"Let us loosen the rope," Johnny said.

The boys had to pull and tug to remove the rope of vines. They inspected it carefully to see if it was badly worn. The noose which had been around the rock showed signs of wear, but not enough to be a danger.

Soon they were lucky to see a strong finger of rock jutting out from near the brow of the cliff. There was no ledge but, from its position, the boys thought they would be able to climb to the top. The face of the cliff at that point was very rugged but did not seem as steep as it was lower down.

Tommy and Johnny felt that, by using their fingers and toes, they could manage to scramble along the rest of the way.

This time, it was Tommy who cast the rock above them. Then he pulled himself up to it. He found that the slope had become less steep but that there were many loose stones around. He saw too that there wasn't enough room at that point for both Johnny and himself. He would have to reach the crest before Johnny climbed up.

Tommy found a foothold in a small crevice in the rock. Into this he hooked his toes. He could not look down, because the front of his body was pressed against the cliff.

"Johnny, don't come up yet!" he called, as he felt a tug on the rope. "There isn't enough space for the two of us."

"I think so!"

Tommy stopped talking. He knew he had to save all his breath for the rest of the climb. Although it was rapidly becoming darker, he also knew he should not hurry. He would have to be slow and sure. Stretching his arms full length, he felt around him with his fingers. He found places to grip, and hauled himself up, feeling with his toes for holes in the rock. Slowly, inch by inch, he made his way upwards. He was almost at the top now. He soon found what he thought to be a piece of rock strong enough to bear his weight. While he hung on, seeking a ledge for his toes, the piece of rock in his left hand gave way.

His body jerked downward. The fingers of his right hand could not hold his weight. They began to slip! He heard Johnny cry out below. Clutching blindly at the cliff, he managed to find the rope again and hung on for dear life!

Johnny was still calling out to him, but he could not reply at once. He was panting as if he had just been under water. His arms and shoulders felt as if they were being torn apart.

"Hold on, Tommy!" shouted Johnny from below. "Hold on! I'm coming!"

But it would be worse if Johnny had come up. There was not enough room on the rock-face for both of them.

"No, Johnny, don't!" he said with an effort, "I'll manage!"

Tommy waited until he had rested a bit. Then, slowly, painfully, he began to climb again. He tested every hold before trusting himself to it. He groaned each time he moved.

At last the young warrior clambered to the top of the cliff. He hauled himself on to the rough grass and lay there, face downward, unable to move.

CHAPTER ELEVEN

THE MOCHO MAROONS

Tommy heard Johnny anxiously calling his name. He opened his eyes, raised his head and found that night had overtaken them. Springing to his feet, he crouched at the edge of the cliff. He could barely see Johnny in the starlight.

"I'm all right, Johnny!" he called.

"I've been calling you for some time! I thought something had happened to you!"

"No. I was just tired," Tommy said.

"I'm coming up now," Johnny said.

But Tommy remembered what had nearly happened to him near the end of his climb. In the dark, Johnny was almost sure to fall. He could not allow his friend to take the risk.

"No, Johnny, wait," he said. "I know what I'll do."

Tommy went into the bush. Using his knife, he cut from a guava tree a long branch with a crook. He returned to the edge of the cliff, lay flat and reached downward with this crook. Catching the rope, he pulled it up to him. After a few tugs, he loosened the noose from the rock. He then tied one end of the rope to a strong old tree growing near by. He threw the other end down to Johnny. In another few minutes, both boys were together on the top of the cliff.

They were too weary to do much talking. They just wanted to sleep for hours. But there was work to be done. The whole village was depending on them to bring help.

They picked some ripe guavas, and set off again. Like all other young warriors, they knew how to guide themselves by the stars. They marched westwards through the forest, and at moonrise they were crossing a clearing. There was a strangely shaped mountain ahead of them. It looked like one of the loaves of sugar which the Maroons used to make. Johnny pointed to it.

"Yes, that's the mountain Chief Phillip told us about," Tommy said.

Aching in every joint and hardly able to keep their eyes open, both boys stumbled on. They felt that they had to keep going. They, as young warriors, had given their promise to the Mountain Top villagers. They had said they would get through, and were determined to do so.

"Perhaps we should sound the abeng now," Johnny said.

They stopped and Tommy brought the horn to his lips. He sent out the call for help. The long, low moan went over the countryside. It rose higher and higher and went down again until it dropped and then ceased slowly. They could hear its echoes far away.

The boys took turns to sound the call for help. Around them lay the forest, bathed in moonlight. The great trees stood without movement. A few frogs croaked. The boys stood close to each other, watching all around them. They knew that they were now deep in Maroon land and that the eyes of others could be on them. They stood and waited.

Then they heard a voice.

"Who are these young strangers who sound the abeng in the dead of night?"

The boys could not tell exactly from where the voice came. It could have come from the earth or from the tops of the trees. They stood perfectly still. Then Tommy spoke.

"We are young warriors sent on a mission by Chief Phillip of Mountain Top," he said proudly.

"Ho, a little rooster!" said the voice.

"Two of us," said Johnny boldly. A young warrior should never seem afraid.

"And yet, my two little roosters walk through the forest like two foolish ducks, not looking to see whether an enemy was on their trail."

"We knew you would be near," said Tommy, "but we also know that when a Maroon warrior does not want to be seen, not even the trees can know where he is."

Laughing softly, the Maroon warrior stepped out of the shadows. He was not wearing his bush dress, yet, standing beside the tree, he had been such a part of the forest that the boys did not see him.

"I am John, scout of the Mocho Maroons," he said. "What is the message from Chief Phillip?"

"We bear a message from Chief Phillip to the Chief of the Mocho Maroons," Tommy said. "We were not told that the message should be given to a scout."

"Hmm," the scout said, after a pause, "not foolish ducks, but two clever roosters. Very well. Follow me."

He stepped off lightly, walking quickly through the forest. The boys went swiftly after him. Like many other scouts, he carried no musket, but was armed only with a bow and a cutting spear. A scout should go silently about his business and muskets made too much noise.

The scout was walking too fast for the weary boys. They found that they could not keep up with him. He halted to wait for them.

"What is this? Are young Mountain Top warriors not taught to walk through the forest?"

"We are very tired," Johnny said sharply. He did not like to be mocked.

The scout looked more closely at them.

"When did you begin your journey?" he asked.

"Before the moon rose last night," Tommy said.

"What? You came over the cliff?"

"Yes," Tommy said.

"No wonder you're tired," the warrior said softly. "You should be ready to drop."

"We are," Tommy said. "Right here."

The warrior thought for a while. Then he put his fingers between his lips and whistled. His action was so sudden that the boys nearly jumped. It was not long before he was joined by another warrior. Like John, this one stepped suddenly from behind a tree.

"This is my brother scout," John said.

"Greetings," the boys said politely.

"Welcome," the new scout said.

"These are two young warriors from Mountain Top. There is some trouble there," John said. "They began their journey before the moon rose last night."

"Before the moon rose?" the newcomer asked, as if he could not believe it.

"They are weary. They bear messages from their chief to our chief. We should get them to him quickly," John said.

Before the boys knew what was happening, they were

picked up and being carried swiftly through the forest by the two scouts. They were too tired even to protest.

Before entering the village, they were stopped twice by guards of the Mocho camp. With all haste, Tommy and Johnny were taken to the Council-hut where they sat on a mat and waited.

The boys stood when the chief of the Mocho Maroons came in. He was a slim man, with broad shoulders. He seemed younger than Chief Phillip.

"Greetings, O Chief," the boys said.

"Welcome," the Chief said.

"We bring messages to you from Chief Phillip of Mountain Top," Tommy said.

"Speak on, boy."

"Chief Phillip says that we should tell Chief James that the Redcoats are on him with their swivel guns. He feels that he may have to fall back deeper into the mountains.

Yet, if he could have the help of Chief James and his famous Mocho warriors, he would wipe out the Redcoats."

Chief James thought in silence for a moment.

"What of the village of Mountain Top?" he asked.

"Chief Phillip says that if needs be, he will put it to the torch and burn it," answered Tommy.

As he spoke, the boy tasted the salt tears in his throat. He had been born in the village and loved it dearly.

"He will burn it," Chief James said softly, "to go wandering again; to hide deeper and deeper in the mountains."

"He says he will destroy it like Nanny Town," Johnny said, blinking back his own tears. For he, like Tommy, loved his little village of Mountain Top, with its streams and green grass and its fields, full of ripe peas and yams.

"Very well. You two young warriors may take some rest. I hear that you left your village before the moon rose last night. Fine lads! Get some rest while I hold a council-meeting."

"Please sir, I would like to say something more," Tommy said.

The Chief listened keenly while Tommy told him of Charlie. Then he shook his head.

"It seems Chief Phillip has all the bravest boys in the mountains," Chief James said. "We'll have to see what's to be done. Do you think that this boy, Charlie, will tell the Redcoats how to find your village?"

"We don't know, sir. We know he is brave, but the English may torture him," Tommy said.

"That's all the more reason why we must hurry," said Chief James. "We can't tell what he may do when he is made to suffer pain."

CHAPTER TWELVE

CAPTURED BY THE REDCOATS

CHARLIE was not sure why he had followed Tommy and Johnny from Mountain Top. He had been frightened when he knew that Tommy had found out that he had cheated in the race to Lookout Rock. He had been afraid that perhaps Chief Phillip also knew about it. Confused by his fear, he had trotted into the bush behind the warriors whom Captain Dick led from the village. He had stuck to their trail. When Captain Dick met the scout, Peter, Charlie had been hiding in the bush close to them. During the Maroons' attack on the sleeping Redcoats, he had been waiting, hidden in the forest. He had seen when the tall Redcoat fired at Tommy and Johnny. Crawling on his belly through the grass, Charlie had managed to cross the valley while the English camp was in a state of confusion. Then he had set off after the boys.

Sobbing with misery for most of the way, Charlie had a faint hope that perhaps he could somehow help the boys. Not only would this make him feel better, but it might also cause his friends to forgive him. Charlie, fearing that the other boys had heard Tommy's remark to him, could hardly face them again.

He had seen the boys escape from the boar and had been in hiding when the soldiers came up. The rest of it we know.

Now he was struggling with the fat soldier and shouting with all the power of his lungs.

"Stop fighting, or I'll knock you on the head!" yelled the Redcoat.

Of course the soldier was too strong for Charlie and soon had the boy in his power. He twisted Charlie's arm behind his back, and the boy cried out in pain. The other Englishman was sitting on the ground, rubbing his ankle and moaning. They were both very angry that Tommy and Johnny had stolen their muskets.

"All right, you come along with me," said the fat soldier, after Charlie had stopped struggling.

Gripping the boy's arm tightly, he pushed him ahead forcing him to trip forward on his toes.

"Where did those boys suddenly come from?" said the fat soldier to his companion.

The tall one shook his head, his face still twisted with pain.

"Don't know. They must have been hiding in the bush. I suddenly saw them running towards our muskets. I grabbed at them but they had some greasy stuff on their skins and slipped from my hands. Then, one of them struck my ankle."

"Is it broken?"

"I don't think so, but it's in bad shape." He looked angrily up at his comrade. "If you had not been so greedy for meat, this would not have happened."

"No need to yell at me. We at least caught one of them."

As the tall soldier looked at him, Charlie felt smaller than a beetle. He was terribly afraid. He was sure that they would show him no mercy.

"Get me a stone so I can break every bone in his body," said the tall man.

"No, we won't kill him yet. The captain will want to talk to him. He can lead us to the Maroon village."

Charlie began to sob. He could not help it. His arm felt as if it was being torn from his body.

"Then tie him up, and help me with my leg," the tall one growled.

Charlie's arms were tied behind him by the leather strap from the water-bottle of one of the soldiers. Afterwards he was thrown to the ground.

The tall soldier still seemed to be in pain. He took off his boot, exposing a badly swollen ankle. He groaned as his comrade bandaged it with strips of cloth torn from his shirt. Both men continued to talk in angry tones. They swore about what they would do to Charlie when they returned with him to their camp. The boy, hearing this, tried to crawl away. With a swing of his hand, the tall soldier struck Charlie a hard blow on the mouth.

The boy cried out. His mouth started to bleed and a tooth was loosened.

"You try that again and I will knock you down," the Redcoat bellowed.

They made their way back to camp, pushing Charlie ahead of them. The Maroon boy knew that, even if he made a dash into the forest, he could not run very fast with his arms lashed behind him.

They went past the Redcoat sentry and were greeted with shouts as the soldiers saw them. Charlie was taken into the presence of the captain. He stood with his head down while the two Redcoats explained what had happened.

"I should have you both court-martialled for allowing a couple of Maroon boys to get the better of you," the captain, a stout, red-haired man with a fierce moustache, said angrily.

Turning to Charlie, he asked in a thundering voice, "Where were you going, boy?"

"No—no—nowhere, sir," stammered Charlie, frightened almost out of his wits.

"You are lying!" shouted the captain.

The captain put his hand on the hilt of his sword. Charlie thought that the fierce man was about to draw it and plunge it into him. His knees began to knock together.

"To—to—hunt—we were going on a hunt!" he cried out.

The captain looked at him without saying a word. Then he shook his head.

"You are lying. No Maroon would be hunting around these parts knowing that we were up in the mountains. There was something peculiar about that attack this morning. The Maroons were trying to pull us away from here. They did not want to fight, but just to have us follow them. Why did they want to lead us away from here?" he roared.

Charlie was dumb. To the boy the captain seemed like an angry giant, ready to eat him up.

"Was it to get you boys past us? Was that it? Have the Maroons sent for help?" roared the giant.

Charlie was too terrified to reply. He wished he could shrink into the ground. He wanted to run away but the hated Redcoats were all around him. The brass buttons on their chests hurt his eyes. He could smell the leather they wore and see their big, red faces turned towards him.

The captain brought his face closer to Charlie's.

"We shall soon loosen your tongue," he said in a terrible whisper.

With his eyes still fixed on Charlie's he snapped a finger at one of his soldiers.

"Soldier, build me a fire and heat some irons red hot. We will warm the roots of his tongue and see if that will make him talk," he said.

Charlie whimpered. His knees gave way and he fell to the ground.

"Hurry up with that fire!" the captain shouted savagely as he began to unbuckle his sword.

CHAPTER THIRTEEN

TO THE RESCUE

Tommy and Johnny had been given a meal of warm milk and bammy. They had stretched themselves out on the floor of a hut and had at once fallen to sleep. When at last they were awakened by John, the scout, they could not tell how long they had slept. They followed John back to the Council-hut where Chief James and his councillors were assembled. The street in Mocho was now filled with Maroons among whom were warriors armed and ready to march.

Then Chief James said to Tommy and Johnny, "Our warriors are leaving for Mountain Top. I shall send and tell your parents that their two brave young warriors are safe and well. Is there anything else you would like us to tell them?"

The boys looked at each other and a swift, silent conversation seemed to pass between them.

"But, sir!" cried Tommy. "We want to go with the warriors! We must rescue Charlie and help to fight for our village!"

Chief James frowned.

"You boys are tired. You cannot keep up with the march."

"But we can, Chief. We had a very long rest," cried Johnny. "Moreover, we can show you where we hid the two fine English muskets."

A roar of laughter came from the Council-men.

"We can really use these two fine English muskets," the Chief said, "but believe me, you did not sleep very long, my young rooster—only for a few minutes."

"We are used to very little sleep, sir," Tommy said quickly.

"Very well. We thought you would want to go back. But promise me that you will do whatever the war captain tells you."

The boys promised.

The warriors left before daylight. Tommy and Johnny soon found what the Chief had meant when he said they should do as they were told. For as soon as they had left the village, two warriors picked up the boys and swung them to their shoulders. The boys cried out that they

97

would prefer to walk like the other warriors, but the war captain only laughed.

"You would not be able to keep up with us. You did your share of walking last night, and yesterday, and the night before."

"We don't want to be carried!" Tommy said. "We are young warriors!"

"And as young warriors, you will remember that you cannot break a promise. You promised Chief James to do as you were told," the war captain said.

It was not long before the boys saw that he was right. The Mocho warriors moved so rapidly that they could never have kept up with them.

The Mocho soldiers did not go down the face of the cliff. They had a secret way which took them through the holes in the Talking Rock, until they entered a cave. Led by men bearing torches they walked for a long time through caves, each of which was a picture of beauty in the light of the torches. Rivers had once flowed through them cutting lovely lace-like patterns into the rocks. The sight thrilled Tommy and Johnny for never before had they seen anything so wonderful. In Mountain Top there were only small caves in which wild boars sometimes lived.

The caves led out to the tall grass which the boys had crossed the day before.

The group reached the river by early afternoon. The scouts who had been sent ahead reported that there were no Redcoats near by.

"Get out the boats," the war captain ordered.

The boys' eyes bulged when they saw what happened next. Using the blades of their swords and cutlasses, the Mocho Maroons scraped away the soft river mud near the root of a big cotton tree. There, packed with rushes to keep it clean inside, was a large canoe. It was a dug-out that had been made from one large cotton tree.

"Where did this come from?" Tommy asked one of the warriors.

He laughed at the look of wonder on Tommy's face and said, "This is used for fishing, boy. We hide it here from the Redcoats. When we want to fish, we just take it up and sail off. Then when we return we cover it up again."

With a couple of men rowing the boat back and forth, the warriors crossed the river and took to the forest. On they went, swiftly but quietly. The boys spoke to the war captain when they reached the place where they had hidden the muskets. There was no cheering, for everyone had to be quiet, but the warriors looked at Tommy and Johnny with respect. They grinned and shook their heads.

As they neared the valley in which the Redcoats had encamped, the Mocho army halted. They sent their scouts ahead to find the Mountain Top men.

The Maroons did not make camp as the Redcoats would have done. They did not sit around in the open. The war captain just held up his hand, palm out, and brought it down sharply. The warriors suddenly sank out of sight. It was as if the earth had swallowed them.

The company lay in high grass and thicket until dusk. Then, at a low whistle from their captain, they were out again, ready to march. Before setting out, they waited until their scouts had returned. Not long afterwards they joined up with the Mountain Top men.

CHAPTER FOURTEEN

CAPTAIN DICK AGREES

"Has there been a battle since we left?" Tommy asked his father.

"No, son. Just a little firing but not a real battle."

"Then we are in time," Tommy said.

He lay beside his father at the root of a pimento tree. The two Maroon armies had encamped in the middle of a forest while the chiefs held a council-of-war. Scouts had been placed all around the camp. The men spoke in whispers. No fires were lit.

"It was a very brave and fine thing you and Johnny did," his father said. "Chief Phillip is proud of you. And so are we. This deed shall be put into song one day, just as your mother said."

"We were frightened most of the time, father."

"People are bravest when they are afraid and still do their duty."

"Charlie must be very frightened still," Tommy said. He had never ceased to think of Charlie. He thought of him as a prisoner in the camp of the Redcoats, and shivered.

His father stirred, putting the sword which was strapped on his hip in a more comfortable position.

"I want to tell you something," he said quietly.

"Yes, father."

"Tommy, Chief Phillip and some of us Council-men

knew that Charlie had cheated on the run to Lookout Rock."

Tommy was very surprised.

"How—how—did you know?" he stammered.

"We are Maroons. We know the mountains. Charlie was not tired enough when he came in. Nor did he wipe his mouth clean enough. We saw that he had eaten."

The boy lay still. So the Chief had known all along. What would they do now? Would they leave Charlie in the hands of the English?

"Is Chief Phillip going to leave him to be killed by the Redcoats?" Tommy asked fearfully.

"We cannot spare warriors to rescue Charlie. This is a war, son. We must save the village. We must think of the greater number of people," his father said.

Tommy sat up.

"But Charlie saved the whole village! The Redcoats would have caught Johnny and me if he had not suddenly appeared."

His father sighed. He knew that what Charlie had done was his duty. But he also knew that Tommy was not thinking of this. The boy was thinking of his friend's safety.

"What we fear is that, although Charlie tried to save the village then, he may have betrayed it by now. We don't think Charlie will be brave enough to stand whatever punishment the English will give to him."

"What do you mean?" asked Tommy.

"I mean he may lead the English soldiers to Mountain Top," his father said.

"He will not!" Tommy whispered furiously. "When he saved Johnny and me, he was brave!"

His father was silent for a while. Then he sighed again.

"Yes, Tommy. Charlie was very brave. I don't know what I would do if he was my friend. Perhaps I would take the other young warriors and go to see Captain Dick. He is the war captain," his father said softly.

Tommy rose silently. He crept about the camp, giving the three croaks of a frog as he went. One by one, he was joined by Johnny, David and Uriah. He told them what his father had said. They talked it over and decided what they should do.

"Let us go and see Captain Dick," Tommy suggested.

They met the war captain coming from the council-of-war.

"Please, Captain Dick," Tommy said.

Captain Dick stopped. He peered at the four shadows standing on the edge of the track.

"Who are you? What are you doing here? Why are you not with the other warriors?" he asked sharply.

"We were coming to see you, Captain Dick," Tommy told him.

"Is that Tommy? And are those the young warriors with you?"

"Yes, Captain Dick. We would like to know when we are going to rescue Charlie, sir," Tommy said.

"Not until after the attack, boy. We cannot spare the warriors now."

Captain Dick spoke more kindly now, because he knew how worried the boys were.

"The *attack*, sir? Are we going to *attack* the Redcoats?" Johnny asked in surprise. The other boys were surprised too, for the Maroons hardly ever attacked a strong body of troops. The practice was to lead the English soldiers into an ambush.

"Yes. The English soldiers will not expect us to attack them."

"But won't we lose too many men in that way, sir? Won't most of our people be killed? Why don't we lead them into an ambush?" Tommy asked.

Captain Dick took a long time to answer. He cleared his throat and, when he spoke, his voice was low.

"For two reasons, and I will tell you because I think you ought to know. You have done well for the village, and, besides, a part of what I have to say has to do with Charlie. The first reason is that the Redcoats will not carelessly walk into an ambush now. They know that yesterday morning we were leading them away for a purpose. They may have guessed that purpose by now. After their meeting with Tommy, Johnny and Charlie, they may have supposed that we were sending for help."

The boys said nothing. They waited anxiously to hear the second reason, for it concerned Charlie.

"The other reason is this. The English may force Charlie by torture to lead them to our village. If he does, we may never have the chance of making an ambush. They will be taking their swivel guns with them and, unless we have the right place for a trap, they will blow us to pieces. The only place where we could trap them and where they could not use their swivel guns, would be Starapple Gully."

The boys knew the Gully which was famous for its many star-apple trees and the wild pigs which went there to feed. It was a very good spot for an ambush, for there were thick forests on both sides. The bottom, an old river bed, was sandy. The English soldiers would find it very hard to fight there, for the Maroons would be among the trees firing at them from either side.

"Sir, but suppose we could get Charlie out before he leads the soldiers to the village?" Johnny asked.

"We cannot spare the men. Besides, the English camp will be very much on the watch tonight."

Suddenly, an idea came to Tommy.

"But we could get him out, Captain Dick!" he said excitedly. "We young warriors could go in without being seen! Then you would have no need to use your warriors!"

The boys moved closer to Tommy. They held their breath and waited for Captain Dick to reply.

They felt sure that they could get into the English camp without being seen.

Captain Dick thought the matter out. He was as anxious as Tommy and his friends to rescue Charlie. Whatever wrong Charlie had done before, he had made up for it. It would be a great risk for the boys to take, but as Maroons they would have to take risks all their lives.

Captain Dick looked through the trees at the stars. They had not yet begun to disappear.

"You will have to do it before the moon rises," he said.

"Before the moon rises," Tommy repeated.

"Very well, young warriors," Captain Dick said softly.

CHAPTER FIFTEEN

OUTWITTING THE REDCOATS

THE young warriors set off at a lope, which was a pace between a walk and a trot. The mountain men were famous for their lope, by which they could go fast and for long distances.

The boys wore only their pantaloons and their knives. They had left their shirts, bows and arrows at the Maroon camp. The ointment of herbs had been rubbed on their half-naked bodies. They went rapidly but silently downhill, keeping to the trees, always on the alert for any scouts the English may have sent.

They had covered about four miles, when they saw the

first glimmer of the English camp fires through the trees. Tommy, who was in the lead, halted the boys by croaking like a frog. Tommy tightened the goatskin belt which held his pantaloon at the waist. He touched each of his companions, and they bent their heads towards him.

"Two of us will go in, and two will remain on watch. If the two who enter are caught, then the others must go back and report to Captain Dick," he said.

"Which two will go in?" David asked.

"I'll be one. We'll choose another to go with me. Let us pick him by the stone-leaf-knife game. David and Johnny will begin," replied Tommy.

David turned to face Johnny. At a tap from Tommy, both spoke at once.

"Stone," said David.

"Knife," said Johnny.

"Stone blunts knife, so David wins," Tommy said. "Now it's the turn of David and Uriah. Ready. Now!"

"Leaf," said Uriah.

"Leaf," said David at the same time.

Both boys had spoken together. The boys laughed softly. Although there was danger ahead, they were still cheerful.

"Ready once more. Now!" said Tommy.

"Leaf," said David again.

"Stone," said Uriah.

"Leaf wraps up stone, so David wins. David will come with me," Tommy said.

Quickly they were off. Johnny and Uriah stopped at the edge of the valley. Tommy and David went on, keeping a sharp look-out for English sentries.

At first, the two boys crouched as they walked; but, as they descended the valley nearer to the camp fires, they dropped to their bellies and began to crawl. They came to a great rock and stopped behind it.

"I'll look to the right. You look to the left and see

whether we can find where they have placed Charlie," Tommy said to David.

They peered cautiously around the rock on either side. The soldiers were camped in the open because the weather was fine. Otherwise they would be in tents. There were three fires in the camp. Each fire had a number of soldiers around it. The boys saw the sentries standing just outside the ring of light around the camp. There were four of them, one at each angle, in a sort of rough square. The soldiers were having their evening meal.

Because of the unevenness of the ground, there were large areas of shadow which the light from the fires did not reach. It was near one of these that they saw Charlie.

Charlie, with his hands tied behind him, was being fed by a soldier. The Redcoats were making fun at him; for the soldier often poked too much food into his mouth, and whenever he choked, the men laughed. Tommy and David ground their teeth in anger.

"Perhaps one of us could get close enough to cut his bonds," David said.

Charlie was sobbing. They could see his shoulders shaking as he wept; they knew that he was frightened and lonely.

"We have to get him out," Tommy said.

"The trouble is that while we are trying to get him out, one of the soldiers may see us," David replied.

"If only we had a way of attracting their attention to something else," Tommy said, "I could slip forward in the shadow and cut his bonds."

Then he heard David chuckling softly beside him.

"What's the joke?" he whispered angrily.

"I know a way to turn their eyes from Charlie," David said; "and all you will have to do is to cut his bonds. Just watch me. And when you are ready with Charlie, croak three times, like a frog."

"What are you going to do?" demanded Tommy.

"I'll tell them an endless story about an endless hurricane. Then when you have cut him loose and crawled back into the bush, just croak three times in the way we signal to each other."

David went without another word to Tommy, for he knew that Tommy would have tried to stop him. To Tommy's horror, he began walking towards the camp fires. Even before the sentries saw him, David had begun to—sing.

Tommy was dumbfounded. Had David gone mad?

David sang a wild Maroon song at the top of his voice. He walked towards the camp fires as if he had not an enemy in the world. One of the sentries shouted to him to stop, but David walked on. The sentry aimed his musket at him, but David continued to sing. Suddenly a loud command rang out and an officer stood near the smallest fire. The sentry lowered his musket and David strode on, singing his hunting song. Not even once did he look towards Charlie, and he ended his song only when he was near the fires. He halted in such a position that all eyes, turned away from Charlie to stare at him. Holding his hands above his head, he cried out, "Greetings, O mighty Redcoats!"

For a moment, there was silence. Then a roar of anger came from the captain.

"Bring me that boy!" he bellowed, his fierce moustache twitching.

Two soldiers grabbed David but they had no need to drag him to the captain, for the boy walked nimbly over. He bowed gracefully.

"Who are you? What do you want?" shouted the captain.

"Sir, my name is David, and I am a Maroon, a singer of songs and a teller of Anancy stories. I was in the forest and saw the fires of the great Redcoats. So I came down to tell my Anancy stories in the hope that the English, who are famous for their kindness, will give me a coin and a meal."

"A Maroon come to an English camp for a meal? You must be a lunatic! Ho! Ho! Ho!" roared the captain with laughter.

The soldiers joined in the laughter, but while they were laughing, David had thrown back his head and his eyes rolled upward. His face shone like polished ebony in the light of the fire, and his pleasant-sounding voice reached their ears.

"Once upon a time there were some soldiers of the King, and they wore bright red coats. They were brave men whose deeds were often told in song. And these brave men were the new Jamaicans who ruled the land from sea to sea."

One after another, the soldiers stopped laughing to listen to the golden voice, and look at the beautiful black face of the youth gleaming like a coal on fire in the light.

Tommy's heart almost stopped. But, knife in hand, he crawled on through the darkness, his eyes fixed on the back of Charlie's head. He did not know how long David could carry on his story. But he remembered that the good Anancy story-teller could keep adding to his tale almost as long as he wished.

"The brave men of England ruled the island from sea to sea. But the men of Africa, who became the Maroons, set up their kingdom on the mountains," David continued.

He moved about as he talked, making motions with his hands. His sharp eyes had already seen that, if he kept strolling about while he talked, there were times when he would be near to a thick coco bush. A plan had already formed in his mind.

"Now, one day in the middle of the year, there was a hurricane. This hurricane began early one morning and it blew all day, and blew down the house Brer Anancy had built. Now Brer Anancy was very sad. For you see, while the brave men of England ruled the land from the seas of the east to the seas of the west, and while the brave Maroons ruled the mountain land from the great Blue Mountains in the east to the Dolphin Head Mountains in the west, all Brer Anancy wanted to rule was his house that he had built! And this was the first hurricane."

By this time, Tommy had reached Charlie. The soldier who had been poking the food in his mouth, had left to join the others who were standing around David. Worming his way through the grass, Tommy stopped just behind Charlie. Now he was lying in the dark but his friend who was sitting up had his face in the light. Charlie's mouth was wide open as he gazed in wonder at David telling his story to the Redcoats. Now and then Charlie jerked forward but Tommy didn't know why he did so.

Suddenly Charlie gave a jump as he heard in a whisper behind him, "Charlie—don't look behind you! It's me, Tommy!" He began to turn his head, then kept still.

"Tommy, oh, Tommy!" he said, with a sob.

"We have come for you. I'm going to set you free," whispered Tommy again.

"No, don't! Look—around my neck!" gasped Charlie.

Tommy looked and almost shouted. Now he knew why Charlie's body had jerked every now and then. Around Charlie's neck was a rope, and Tommy saw that the end was held by a soldier. Even as Tommy looked, the soldier turned around and pulled at the rope to make sure Charlie was there. The boy's head flapped forward like a chicken on a string.

"I will cut the rope and we can run for the forest. They won't be able to aim very well in the firelight," Tommy said.

"No, Tommy. I cannot go with you."

"Why? You will be safe again!" whispered Tommy.

"I cannot return to Mountain Top. I've betrayed my people."

"What did you tell the Redcoats?" asked Tommy.

"Everything. I told them how many men were in the village and how Chief Phillip had sent for help from Mocho. I told them how to get to the village and promised to lead them there," said Charlie in a low voice, the tears running down his cheek.

"But why, Charlie? Why did you?"

"Because they held red-hot irons at my cheek and chest!" wept Charlie. "I—I—was afraid!"

"Yes. I would be afraid too," said Tommy.

"The Redcoats will be marching as soon as the moon

comes up," Charlie said. "Go back and tell Chief Phillip."

"Then I will cut the cord now. You can run back with us and tell Chief Phillip. He will be able to move all our people before the Redcoats come."

"But I cannot return, Tommy. I am a traitor. I'll have to stay with the Redcoats," cried Charlie.

"But the Redcoats will kill you!" Tommy said.

"No. They said they would not if I led them to the village."

"Chief Phillip has made up his mind to attack the English," Tommy said.

Charlie gave a half-cry.

"But—he cannot attack the English! Even with the Mocho men, he could not attack the English and win! They would wipe us out with their swivel guns!" Charlie raised his voice in his excitement.

"Sshh! The Redcoats will hear you," warned Tommy.

He did not want to say that Captain Dick was afraid that Charlie might lead the English to the village, and had therefore decided to attack first.

"Perhaps, if I go back with you, the Redcoats will not be able to find the village quickly," Charlie said, after a moment's thought.

"And we shall be able to escape to the mountains."

"But I'll always be ashamed to know that I had betrayed my people. No! I cannot return with you, but I can lead the Redcoats into an ambush."

"There is no place for an ambush between here and the village," said Tommy impatiently.

"I know," Charlie said calmly. "But let us think of a place and then you can go back and tell Chief Phillip that I'll lead the English to that place."

"Charlie!" gasped Tommy.

"The place. Where should I lead them? Speak quickly before the Redcoat comes back to look at me."

"Star—Starapple Gully!" gasped Tommy.

"Then hurry back now. Tell Chief Phillip that I'll lead them there."

The tears ran down Charlie's cheeks and his shoulders shook.

"No, Charlie. You come back with us," Tommy said.

Charlie shook his head stubbornly, although the tears continued to flow.

"Go back quickly—Starapple Gully," he said between sobs.

The Redcoat pulled at the rope again and jerked Charlie forward. Tommy began to crawl backwards, keeping in the hollows in the ground where the shadows rested. He croaked loudly.

He could hear David's voice:

"And Brer Anancy came to the door of the house he had built after the fourth hurricane. And he looked all around him at the Redcoat soldiers who had gathered to watch this Brer Anancy who kept building house after house, after each hurricane."

Tommy reached the edge of the forest and croaked loudly again three times. David raised his head. His eyes seemed to pierce right across the camp and through the blackness into the trees which he knew Tommy had reached. His voice rang in the stillness of the night, as he continued his story of the endless hurricanes.

"And Brer Anancy threw back his head, just as I do now, and said, 'Oh, you idle, stupid, red-faced Redcoats, leaving your duties to hear a Maroon boy tell a foolish story that has no end—ha, ha, ha! Ho, ho, ho!'"

Then suddenly David threw himself backward into the thick coco bush, and he was as absent as if he had been chalked on a blackboard and rubbed out.

The Redcoats looked at each other. Slowly, they realised that the boy had outwitted them. With howls of rage they descended on the coco bush. But David, of course, was not there.

CHAPTER SIXTEEN

THE BATTLE

The sun rose above the mountain, and light came through the trees into Starapple Gully. Tommy, with the other three young warriors, had climbed into a leafy cedar tree. They had found strong limbs and lay on them, so that their hands were free to aim their arrows. Parting the leaves before his face, Tommy looked down on the high banks on either side of the gully. He knew the Maroon warriors were down there, in ambush, but it was hard to see them. The night before, when Tommy had returned with the message from Charlie, Chief Phillip had ordered the warriors to take up positions at Starapple Gully.

The two Chiefs and their war captains and Councilmen had listened in silence while Tommy told them what had happened at the English camp.

Then, in a quiet voice, Chief Phillip had said, "There never was a braver boy than Charlie. I am proud of him."

The war captains had commanded that the warriors get quickly into their green clothing. This was the dress for ambush. Tommy had never before seen them so fully covered. They had tied the green branches over their bodies, from head to toe. Then, in a swift march, they had gone to Starapple Gully and taken up their places for the ambush. Looking down now as the sunlight entered the gully, Tommy could not tell them apart from the forest.

Tommy heard a croaking on his left. He turned his head and saw David lying flat on a limb. David grinned at him.

"The English soldiers will surely see your big teeth when they enter Starapple Gully," said Tommy.

"They will think I am a tree with teeth, like the one in the Anancy story," David answered. He croaked at Tommy again.

"I've never heard that Anancy story," said Johnny from the limb above them.

"Once upon a time," David began.

"Once upon a time, there was a war. Shut up!" snapped Uriah, who was beside Johnny.

"How long could you have told that Anancy story last night?" Johnny asked.

"Until I ran out of hurricanes," said David with a laugh.

Tommy looked at him. He still trembled sometimes at the risk David had taken the night before. To have gone into the English camp surrounded by all those terrible red jackets, telling them an Anancy story while all the while he was laughing at them!

A sudden trill of bird-calls came from a section of trees across the gully. There was a great movement among what seemed to be clusters of smaller trees and the boys heard the clicks of muskets being primed. They knew that the bird-calls had come from Captain Dick as a command to the warriors to prime their muskets.

The warriors were lined on both sides of Starapple Gully, which was about a hundred yards long. They had entered the gully at one end from a long, shallow valley. From where the Maroons were in ambush, they could see right across the valley to the trees beyond. It was from among these trees that they hoped to see the Redcoats marching behind Charlie into the ambush.

It was a long wait, but the patience of the Maroons never failed. Nobody stirred. Insects buzzed and droned. A yellow snake wriggled through the sand in the gully, searching for food.

Then they heard the Redcoats coming.

They were as noisy as a herd of cattle, marching with a crunching of boots and a rattle of arms. The boys looked at each other, licked their lips, and grinned. Had it been a band of Maroons coming through the forest, nobody would have heard them.

The boys fixed their eyes on the trees. The noise grew louder. And then the soldiers appeared.

In front of them marched their captain, the early morning sun shining on the badge of his cap and on the brass buttons on his coat. Beside him walked a smaller figure, holding his head high. It was Charlie!

They had taken the bonds from his hands but had left the rope around his neck. One end of it was held by a soldier. As they came out of the trees, the captain said something to Charlie. The Maroon boy pointed ahead, straight to Starapple Gully!

On came the English army, marching across the meadow. Tommy knew that two of the Maroon marksmen, already had their eyes on their targets. After hearing the boys' story last night, Captain Dick had given swift orders. One marksman would be aiming at the captain; the other would be aiming at the man holding the rope around Charlie's neck.

Charlie marched steadily, looking straight ahead. But he knew that Maroon warriors were fingering their weapons among the trees and that soon bullets and arrows would be flying around. The front ranks of the English soldiers were now entering the gully. The heavy sand slowed them up, but they pushed on. Now the swivel guns, dragged by teams of soldiers, were rolling along on their wheels through the sand. The young warriors in the trees had a good look at Charlie as he passed underneath them. One side of his face was swollen. He must have fallen or been struck by his captors.

Silently, Tommy and the others waited for the signal. More and more soldiers passed beneath the tree in which they were hidden, their boots raising the dust in the gully. In their tight red jackets and plumed caps, and with the heavy muskets on their shoulders, they seemed too mighty to be beaten by half-naked Maroon warriors. Marching four abreast, their ranks filled the length of Starapple Gully.

Tramp, tramp, tramp, tramp! Their heavy boots shook the earth.

And then the signal came.

A mighty war whoop from Captain Dick.

The trees on either side of Starapple Gully sprang to life. Muskets boomed. Arrows sang through the air. War cries burst from the throats of the Maroon warriors, as the battle began.

The boys had been watching Charlie. The captain and the soldier who held the rope had fallen at the first volley. Instantly, Charlie dived for the side of the gully where some shrubs were growing. Swift as a coney, the boy disappeared into the shrubbery. Tommy and the young warriors let out a cheer that rose even above the din of the battle. "Ho, ho, for Charlie!" they yelled above the booming muskets. "Hey, hey, hey, for Charlie!"

"Come on. Let us give them something to remember!" yelled Tommy.

The young warriors shot their arrows into the tightly packed ranks of Redcoats. Some fell, staggered up and fell again. Many of them lay still. Others were firing back, but they saw nothing at which to aim. Trying to hide from bullets and arrows, they had no time to mark which were the real trees and which were Maroons in their battledress of branches.

Suddenly, above the noise of battle, came the notes of a bugle. It was the signal for the English soldiers to retreat. A roar went up from the warriors. Brave men themselves, the Maroons knew there were also brave men among the Redcoats. But their captain had fallen, and this had thrown the Redcoats into confusion.

The Redcoats were backing out of the gully, firing their muskets as they went. They were dragging the swivel guns but the confusion and heavy sand made this slow work indeed and they lost many men in the retreat.

Some of the younger warriors wanted to follow the Redcoats into the open meadow but a shout from the two war captains stopped them.

"Back! Back! Into the forest!" roared Captain Dick.

Quickly Tommy swung his bow to his shoulder.

"Charlie! Let us go for Charlie!" he yelled to his companions.

The four young warriors jumped to the ground. As nimble as goats, they clambered down the side of the gully and raced across the sand to where Charlie had disappeared. As they went, they saw his head appear above the shrubs.

"Charlie! Charlie! Come along—into the forest!"

Charlie grinned as they surrounded him. They hurried him up the nearby bank and raced into the wood. Shouting and laughing, they ran with Charlie deep into the forest.

CHAPTER SEVENTEEN

VICTORY

THAT night, there was a great victory celebration in the Maroon village of Mountain Top. The Maroons, tired but happy at their success, sang and danced all night. Many of them had just returned from pursuing the enemy. Captain Dick and the war captain of the Mocho Maroons had led their men very skilfully. Taking a longer road through the forest, but running very fast, they were in the trees waiting for the Redcoats when the English crossed the open valley and once more entered the wood. Then, flitting like shadows from tree to tree, they had shot their silent arrows at the enemy until the English fairly ran down the mountains to Guanaboa Vale. The Maroons had lost a few men, but the toll among the Redcoats was heavy.

The five young warriors sat with Chief Phillip and Chief James on a platform built on the parade-ground. A great bonfire lit up the whole place. Over the fire several wild boars and a whole ox were roasted. There were heaps of roasted yams, sweet potatoes, badoes and bammies. There was a small mountain of fruit. The village band was there and the people made merry with many of the dances of the Old Country of Africa.

At the end of the feast, Chief Phillip rose. He held up his hand for silence.

"My brothers and sisters, we are here to celebrate our victory over the enemy," he said. "It is right that we should, for we have fought a good battle."

A cheer went up. Chief Phillip once more called for silence. "We have fought a good battle, but so have the English. Now that the Spaniards are no longer here, we are the Old Jamaicans and the English are the New. Let us hope that the day will come when we can both live together in peace. If we cannot live together, then the English may have the plains. We shall keep our mountains."

"Our mountains! We shall keep our mountains!" shouted the Maroons.

Then, continuing on a sadder note the chief said, "Now whenever there are brave men on either side, many of them are killed. And that is not good."

All nodded, agreeing with Chief Phillip. There was sadness in some of the Maroon houses where husbands and fathers had been lost.

"As it is, we have nearly lost one of our bravest," the Chief said.

He looked to his right on the platform where Charlie sat among the young warriors.

"We nearly lost our brave young Charlie," Chief Phillip said.

Such a shout went up that even the trees around the village seemed to shake.

"Charlie! Brave Charlie!" cried the Maroons.

Chief Phillip held up his hand.

"And it was only the bravery of all the other young warriors, Tommy, Johnny, David and Uriah, that brought Charlie back to us and saved the village of Mountain Top!" cried Chief Phillip.

"Ho! Ho! Hey! Hey! Hey!" roared the Maroons.

Frightened at the noise that rose from the village of Mountain Top, even the wild boars must have hidden deeper in their dens.